Beyond the Lectionary

A Year of Alternatives to the
Revised Common Lectionary

Beyond the Lectionary

A Year of Alternatives to the Revised Common Lectionary

David Ackerman

Winchester, UK
Washington, USA

First published by Circle Books, 2013
Circle Books is an imprint of John Hunt Publishing Ltd., Laurel House, Station Approach,
Alresford, Hants, SO24 9JH, UK
office1@jhpbooks.net
www.johnhuntpublishing.com
www.circle-books.com

For distributor details and how to order please visit the 'Ordering' section on our website.

Text copyright: David Ackerman 2012

ISBN: 978 1 78099 857 2

A CIP catalogue record for this book is available from the British Library.

Design: Stuart Davies

Printed and bound by CPI Group (UK) Ltd, Croydon, CR0 4YY

We operate a distinctive and ethical publishing philosophy in all
areas of our business, from our global network of authors to
production and worldwide distribution.

CONTENTS

BEYOND THE LECTIONARY

David Ackerman's offering of a fourth "Year D" to the three year cycle of lectionary texts is a gift to preachers and teachers who seek to expand their congregation's exposure and study to texts that are often ignored or even avoided in many congregations today. As one who preaches and teaches from the lectionary, I welcome this new resource for its potential to expand both my students' and my congregation's awareness of often ignored biblical figures such as Rahab, Tamar, and Rehoboam, as well as allowing them to spend significant time in (often short-changed) books like Leviticus and Ecclesiastes. Ackerman's thoughtful interweaving of these texts to fit the church year will assist preachers and teachers in enriching their congregations' repertoire of images of God and the multiplicity of ways the biblical account describes God's interactions with God's people.

Anabel C. Proffitt, Ph.D. Associate Professor of Educational Ministry, Lancaster Theological Seminary

Finally, an additional year of lectionary readings that pushes the preacher to confront many of the "texts of terror" in the Bible. In wrestling with these texts, new opportunities for understanding God's supposed violence as a projection of human violence onto God will emerge, resulting in a deeper appreciation for the creative nonviolence of Jesus the Christ. David Ackerman has orchestrated a masterful symphony of diverse and challenging texts in this volume, and his own commentary is both profound and practical.

Rev. Paul Wrightman, Pastor, Community Church of the Monterey Peninsula, Carmel, California

Preaching is an artistic adventure, integrating imagination, text, inspiration, and congregation. Preachers are challenged to discover new images from ancient texts. This is exactly what Beyond the Lectionary does. It presents a lively alternative vision to the Revised Common Lectionary, an imaginative fourth year in which we meet characters and texts omitted in the three-year lectionary cycle. Preachers will find Ackerman's text challenging, engaging, and inspiring. Not for the timid of heart, *Beyond the Lectionary* enables preachers and congregants alike to hear fresh words that will inspire new creation and heart-felt mission. Preachers who experiment with Ackerman's lectionary variations will never be bored or boring, but alive in their encounter with the ever-fresh words of scripture.

Bruce Epperly, Theologian, pastor, spiritual guide and author of *Holy Adventure: 41 Days of Audacious Living* and *Emerging Process: Adventurous Theology for a Missional Church*

Rev. Ackerman has provided preachers with a resource that addresses two vital needs in contemporary congregations. For parishioners who long for the stories they heard as children, familiar figures such as Noah, Jacob, Moses, David, and Daniel will come to life throughout the year in ways the Revised Common Lectionary does not provide. For those who do not know the Biblical story except from popular culture, this lectionary addition will provide context and detail essential to their understanding of the scope of God's love for humankind. This is an essential book for the preacher who wants to dig more deeply into the rich texts of our forebearers in the faith in a thematic, systematic way.

Rev. Ruth Shaver, Pastor, United Church of Schellsburg (UCC)

Introduction

In the context of the Christian church, a lectionary is a collection of Bible readings designated for use on occasions for worship. For centuries, Christian communities have created and used different lectionaries, but today, the predominant one used by mainline Protestant churches is the *Revised Common Lectionary* (hereafter denoted *RCL*). It is based on the 1969 Roman Catholic lectionary, *Ordo Lectionem Missae* (Order of Readings for the Mass) and is a revision of the *Common Lectionary*, which was composed in 1983. The *RCL* is a cyclical, three-year compilation that was arranged in 1992 by the Consultation on Common Texts, a scholarly group comprised of representatives of various Christian traditions. It has been favorably received by churches around the world, and resources expounding on it are popular and abundant. While some Protestant denominations do not use it, many either recommend or require it in their orders of worship. Because the *RCL* determines what readings many Christians worldwide will hear in worship, its significance is enormous for clergy and laypeople alike. As one who religiously preached on the scriptures in the *RCL* for over fifteen years, I readily identify with pastors who use it.

I think this is true for a number of reasons. I like the fact that the lectionary compels me to preach on texts that I might otherwise ignore. I appreciate the discipline of letting my reflections conform to the rhythms and cadences of the liturgical year instead of imposing my favorite texts on a congregation week after week. I relish the ecumenical nature of the lectionary and the thought that members of my church might be harmoniously comparing notes on the scriptures and sermon with friends from the church down the street. The discipline of lectionary preaching encourages me to practice exegesis (reading *out* of the text) over eisegesis (reading my preconceptions *into* it), and I require students in the Practical Theology course I teach to use it, at least for our class. I admire the *RCL* as a true work of art, a masterful arrangement of texts that justifiably enjoys the global reception it has attained.

I must confess, however, that as I began my sixth cycle using the *RCL*, I started to tire of using the same readings. Even though I saw new things in the texts every three years, I sensed that I was overlooking something important. That something was the vast portion of the Bible that the *RCL* overlooks. It is true that in 2005 the Consultation on Common Texts authored a book selecting texts for every day of the year (titled *Revised Common Lectionary Daily Readings*), but the Biblical ground that it covers on Sunday mornings is still significantly limited. By my calculations, the *RCL* uses 7756 verses of the Bible on Sundays and mainline Protestant holy days over its three-year cycle. That amounts to 24.9 percent of the verses in the Bible. On the one hand, it is a remarkable accomplishment to cover nearly a quarter of the Bible in public worship over a three year period. On the other hand, repeating this cycle over the course of many years leaves preachers and parishioners addressing the same 24.9 percent of the Bible and never engaging the remaining 75.1 percent. Because of this systematic omission, there is a danger that lectionary preachers will foster a "canon within the canon" (or "Bible within the Bible") in their churches. I suspect that at least part of the reason for the difficulties presently facing many mainline Protestant traditions is that they claim the Bible to be authoritative yet ignore vast portions of it in their worship life. Churches can no longer expect that this failure will not have consequences for the faith development of their people. There are too many Biblical gems that the *RCL* passes over, and I believe that it is time to give lectionary preachers the opportunity to read and address more of these on Sunday mornings.

Along with those gems, however, are more difficult passages that are very hard for preachers to face. Some are infamous "texts of terror." Preachers may avoid these passages either because they are offended by them or because they believe that there is no word from God in them. Some people have been so wounded by these texts that hearing them read in public worship is painful. Attempts to domesticate or censor such passages, however, only heighten Biblical ignorance among preachers and parishioners alike. These texts are part of the "collective unconscious" of Christianity; present, like an elephant in the room, but seldom discussed. I believe that the task of preachers is not to avoid these readings but to face them honestly. They may find that, with all due respect to the authority of scripture, they are not preaching *on* these texts as much as *against* them. In other words, they love the Bible enough that they do not blithely accept the text at face value but passionately engage and even oppose it so that the truth of God's word breaks through all cultural chasms. Such a practice as this was discouraged by some of my professors when I was in school, but I am now convinced that church leaders have a moral obligation to do this. Unless Christians begin to intentionally address the difficult scriptures that are omitted by the *RCL*, the Bible risks being adopted into the canon of those atheists who, wishing to discredit Christianity, portray it as a book of horrors. By facing such readings squarely, however, I believe preachers and churches will go a long way to stave off the membership-eroding crisis that superficially pits issues of Biblical authority against concerns for social justice in today's world.

All of this points to how important it is for preachers to interpret scripture critically by exploring the context of a passage and uncovering the principles the author uses before attempting to apply it to today. They will find that the practice of "prooftexting," or taking scripture out of context to prove a point, will not suffice with these readings. Literalists who insist that the Bible is uniformly authoritative for Christians are frequently confronted with passages that are impossible to justify at face value as being God's message for today. Those who espouse such literalism approach the study of scripture from a perspective of emotional, psychological and social resistance. In a world of constant change, they want to view the Bible as an eternal object delivered from God's hand and unassailable by the forces of modernity and post-modernity. This, however, turns the Bible into an idol and fails to account for the fact that while it does contain inspired, timeless principles for Christian living, it is a human work written in a particular time to a particular people in a particular physical and cultural setting. Moreover, the Bible does not point to itself as the object of worship, but to God. Christians who wish to avoid the pitfalls of idolatry and discern God's authoritative voice speaking through scripture will coura-geously engage the Bible in its fullness in order to seek God's will in the world today.

Hoping to exercise more of the fullness of the Bible in my preaching, at the end of my fifteenth year of lectionary preaching, I sought a resource that followed the *RCL's* pattern of textual selection and arrangement but offered new readings. At the time, I found none. It then occurred to me that one could probably mine at least one more year of Biblical texts that would, like the *RCL*, include readings from the Hebrew Bible, Psalms, New Testament/Epistles, and Gospels. While adding a fourth year to the lectionary would break up the harmonious (triune) cycle of years (identified as Years A, B and C in the *RCL*), I surmised that, for the sake of a more exhaustive use of the Bible, a case for having such an alternative would be well-grounded. Encouraged by colleagues and friends, I began to work on *Beyond the Lectionary*.

Beyond the Lectionary is a one-year compilation of readings that offers its users an additional 2266 verses of scripture that are not used on Sundays or mainline Protestant holy days in the *RCL*. This amounts to an extra 7.3 percent of the Bible. While this is somewhat less than the average number of new verses presented in the *RCL* each year (by my calculations, 2585), I have kept both pastors and listeners in mind and opted for quality of selections over quantity of verses. I have learned from experience that when readings are shorter, preachers are inclined to read more of the texts and parishioners are likely to listen to them more attentively. I anticipate that this will be viewed favorably in churches that are seeking opportunities to engage parishioners Biblically and theologically in new and enlivening ways.

In terms of the process of the selecting and arranging of the texts, I attempted to paint something of a canvas with the scriptures. I chose colors and textures that I believed were appropriate to the seasons of the liturgical year, and I arranged the readings by focusing on the two guiding principles of continuity (progressing in order) and complementarity (textual completion or harmony). Because I found that the Psalms and the Gospels were well utilized by the *RCL*, the passages that I selected from them were necessarily shorter than those cited in the Hebrew Bible and New Testament/Epistles. In addition to the Sundays of the liturgical year, I offered texts for such holy days as Epiphany, Ash Wednesday, Maundy Thursday and Christmas Eve. I aimed to exclude passages that were obvious variants (repeated readings) of Sunday selections in the *RCL*. The lone exception to my selection criteria was the Gospel text for Christmas Eve (I could not avoid using Luke 2:1-20 for this). In the hope that readers would enjoy the combinations of texts offered in these pages, I chose Biblical narratives that I firmly believed would be compelling ones for preachers to address and listeners to engage.

In terms of the book's structure, the pattern I adopted was to list the readings for each day and then comment on them. I did this by thematically weaving the readings together in such a way that readers could see how the texts fit with each other. I wrote the commentaries so that laypeople could appreciate them and pastors could see how a coherent message may be preached from them. These commentaries are not generic interpretations but are specifically designed to accommodate preachers in their sermon preparation. Readers will see different homiletic possibilities in the passages than the ones I mention, but my suggestions should offer preachers a starting point for reflection. I cite numerous scriptures throughout the book, and all of these are excerpted from the *New Revised Standard Version* of the Bible. After the commentaries, I close with a brief prayer for preachers to use as they consider the readings before them.

To get a sense of how the work would be received, I preached on the texts for a year in my home congregation, St. Paul's United Church of Christ in Trauger (Pleasant Unity) PA. I made numerous adjustments based on feedback that I gleaned during the year in which I used them. Preachers may use the book wholly over the course of any year, or selectively at their discretion. They may use it for worship and devotional purposes as well as for study and personal growth. It may even be creatively adapted by Sunday School classes that are looking for a new and different resource. I anticipate a variety of uses for the book and hope to hear about how people in different settings benefit from its readings, commentaries and prayers.

The list of Biblical characters that this book introduces may be new to hearers of lectionary based sermons. Listeners will meet such wildly diverse figures as Rhoda, Ebedmelech, Mephibosheth, Simon Magus and even one talkative donkey. Preachers will hopefully find that the narratives surrounding these figures will transform the lives of their congregations by expanding their Biblical repertoire and introducing new possibilities for understanding scripture. The stories and ideas in these texts offer varied glimpses of God and diverse commentaries on matters of faith and life. As previously suggested, this lectionary is not for the timid. It is not for preachers who are unwilling to use critical skills in interpreting texts, nor is it for those who want every sermon to be happy, innocuous and inoffensive. I believe that courageous preachers who are willing to take the risks involved in preaching on these texts will reap many rewards by using *Beyond the Lectionary*.

I am very grateful to my sister, Diane Callihan, for her outstanding proofreading work and stylistic advice. I am also indebted to the people of St. Paul's United Church of Christ as well as numerous colleagues whose patience, feedback and encouragement were indispensable. Last, but certainly not least, I thank my wife, Marsha, for being such a steadfast source of love and support. I wish readers and preachers God's blessings as they engage these challenging texts, filled as they are with newness, beauty and danger.

Advent

Advent I

Daniel 2:24, 31-49
Psalm 38:15-22
Revelation 3:14-22
Mark 11:12-14, 20-25

The Christian liturgical year begins with Advent (meaning "coming"), a season of awakening and repentance as well as patience and perseverance. Today's reading from Psalm 38 emphasizes these last themes, as the author writes, "But it is for you, O Lord, that I wait; it is you, O Lord my God, who will answer" (v 15). The Gospel text also does this by calling people to persevere in prayer. In today's divided reading from Mark 11, Jesus finds a barren fig tree, and after he curses it, it withers. He uses it as an object lesson to teach his disciples about having faith in God, believing in prayer and showing forgiveness. Those who practice these lessons over time must be both steadfast and patient.

The remaining texts from Daniel 2 and Revelation 3 emphasize the importance of awakening to the insights that God provides. Revelations from God abound in the Advent readings for all three years of the RCL, and the book of Daniel is one of the most important apocalyptic (revelatory) books in the Hebrew Bible. While chapters 7-12 focus heavily on divine visions, chapters 1-6 also offer amazing stories about the prophet Daniel that never arise on Sundays in the RCL. Daniel 2 is an excellent example of such a story, but because it is long, it is abbreviated here. Preachers may preface this reading by noting that the story begins when King Nebuchadnezzar of Babylon has a troubling dream. He searches for someone to tell him both the dream and its interpretation, and when he finds no one, he threatens to kill all the wise men in the kingdom. This is when God reveals the dream and its meaning to Daniel. Today's reading begins as Daniel tells the executioner not to harm the wise men. He then says that Nebuchadnezzar's dream is about a broken statue, and he interprets it as an allegory about kingdoms that will rise after Babylon falls. When the king hears this insightful interpretation, he promotes Daniel in his kingdom. Like Daniel 2, Revelation 3 is also an apocalyptic piece that calls on people to awaken to God's presence among them. The selection for this day is the Spirit's message to the church at Laodicea. In this story, Jesus, as he is revealed to John of Patmos, warns the Laodiceans of the dangers of being lukewarm in their faith. Because they are neither hot nor cold, he threatens to spit them out of his mouth. Such a message serves as a powerful "wake-up" call to the church, both then and now.

Preachers may experience a sense of dissonance between today's themes and the events in the world around them. The liturgical year is just beginning while the calendar year is drawing to a close. The Biblical texts are apocalyptic and challenging, while the cultural marketplace is saturated with messages of happy holidays. In churches, these difficult readings may be accompanied by such activities as Advent wreath lighting, "Hanging of the Greens" celebrations and/or Holy Communion. During this busyness, however, today's texts challenge parishioners to evaluate their priorities and consider whether they are hot or cold in their faith.

Prayer: God of changing years, help us in these challenging times to be people who watch and wait for you faithfully. Amen.

Advent 2
Daniel 3:19-30
Psalm 57:8-11
Revelation 11:15-19
Luke 1:5-20, 57-66

The readings for this day continue to proclaim Advent messages of awakening and repentance. The texts use sounds and music to awaken their readers to God's coming among them. In Psalm 57, the psalmist cries, "Awake, my soul! Awake, O harp and lyre! I will awake the dawn" (v 8). The selection from Revelation 11 begins with John of Patmos declaring, "Then the seventh angel blew his trumpet, and there were loud voices in heaven, saying, 'The kingdom of the world has become the kingdom of our Lord and of his Messiah, and he will reign forever and ever'" (v 15). All of the vivid sounds in these readings should capture the attention of listening parishioners.

Today's other texts use sounds to emphasize the Advent theme of repentance. The word repent in Greek means "to change one's mind," and these passages show how God intervenes in people's lives to change their minds. The reading from Daniel 3 relates the story of Shadrach, Meshach, and Abednego in the fiery furnace. Before today's selection begins, King Nebuchadnezzar erects a golden statue and commands that people worship it when music starts to play. Daniel's three friends refuse to do this, and today's reading begins with the king angrily sentencing them to death by burning. When Shadrach, Meschach and Abednego emerge from the flames unharmed, Nebuchadnezzar is astonished and blesses God. He changes his mind about the men and promotes them to positions of authority in Babylon. The Gospel reading also tells a story about a man whose mind is changed. On this second Sunday of Advent, the Gospel texts in all three years of the *RCL* focus on the ministry of John the Baptist, and *Beyond the Lectionary* continues this pattern with a story about John found in Luke 1. In this divided selection, the angel Gabriel appears to a priest named Zechariah and tells him that his aging wife, Elizabeth, will conceive a child. When Zechariah refuses to believe the angel's message, he loses his speech. After the child's birth, Zechariah supports his wife's decision to name the boy John, and he regains his ability to speak. With his doubt removed, he praises God. Both Zechariah and Nebuchadnezzar change their minds and by doing so, also change their speech and their lives.

In the season of Advent, music and speech are powerful ways in which preachers may awaken parishioners to a spirit of repentance, or turning to God. In today's selection from Luke 1, Gabriel says of John, "He will turn many of the people of Israel to the Lord their God. With the spirit and power of Elijah he will go before him, to turn the hearts of parents to their children, and the disobedient to the wisdom of the righteous, to make ready a people prepared for the Lord" (vv 16-17). With all the themes from today's texts, preachers have ample ways to turn their parishioners' attention to the Advent message of God's coming into the world.

Prayer: Awaken us, God, to the ways in which you come to us in this season of new beginnings. Change us, so that we may be faithful in proclaiming your good news. Amen.

Advent 3
Daniel 5:1-7, 17, 25-28
Psalm 62:1-2
Revelation 15:2-4
Matthew 24:15-22

Advent is a season of contrasts. On the one hand, many churches observe it with the lighting of an Advent wreath. On each Sunday in the season, a candle is lit as Christians await God's coming in the birth of Jesus. The author of Psalm 62 emphasizes the importance of such patience by writing, "For God alone my soul waits in silence; from him comes my salvation" (v 1). Also, on this third Sunday in Advent, some traditions observe Gaudete Sunday. The word "Gaudete" is Latin for "rejoice," and on this day, many churches light a rose colored candle (instead of the violet used on the other three Sundays) to symbolize the joy of the season. As many Christians light the candles of the wreath (often used to signify hope, peace, joy and love) and celebrate Christmas pageants and concerts at this time of year, the theme of joy is inescapable.

On the other hand, the handwriting is definitely on the wall when it comes to today's remaining scriptures, and the message that appears in them is one of judgment. Such a theme is consistent with readings for this Sunday from the *RCL*, which also include explicit references to judgment (for example, James 5:7-10 in Year A or Luke 3:7-18 in Year C). Today's readings include a story in Daniel 5 about a mysterious hand writing a cryptic saying on the wall of King Belshazzar's palace. The king is having a party with the vessels from the temple in Jerusalem, and he is terrified when he sees the apparition. Daniel interprets the message on the wall as both an indictment of the king's excessive pride and a prediction of the downfall of Babylon. A similar message of judgment in Revelation 15 falls upon the conquered beast from chapter 13, as the victors stand by a sea of glass and sing God's praise. In their song, they proclaim, "All nations will come and worship before you, for your judgments have been revealed" (v 4). Additionally, the reading from Matthew 24 is a text of judgment in which Jesus connects Daniel's prophecy to the Roman Empire's destruction of the Jerusalem temple. He says, "And if those days had not been cut short, no one would be saved; but for the sake of the elect those days will be cut short" (v 22). Such a message of judgment serves as an exhortation to faithfulness now, while there is still time to change.

While joy and judgment may appear to be incompatible themes, the tension between them reflects the fact that Advent is a season of paradoxes. People anticipate Jesus' birth as Christmas draws near, but today's texts challenge their readers to see that the meaning of this season is about more than the birth of a child. It is about God's coming into the world, with all the wildness and enormity that this entails. As parishioners continue to wait for this event with a mixture of joy and anxiety, preachers will do well to confront the complex realities that these texts and times present.

Prayer: God, as we await your coming in our world, make us attentive to your judgments and fill us with joy and expectation. Amen.

Advent 4
Daniel 6:16-27
Psalm 108:1-5
Revelation 18:1-3
Matthew 23:13-26

The reversal of the world's powers is an important Advent theme which today's reading from Daniel 6 addresses. Preachers will want to set the stage for this story by noting that early in Daniel 6, some leaders who are jealous of Daniel persuade King Darius the Mede to ordain that anyone who prays to a god other than the king will be thrown into a den of lions. They catch Daniel praying to God, and Darius is distressed when he realizes he must follow through with the terms of his own ordinance. Today's reading begins with the king reluctantly commanding that Daniel be thrown into the den of lions. When Daniel emerges unharmed, Darius is relieved. He then throws Daniel's accusers into the lions' den and makes a new decree that all people in his kingdom should worship Daniel's God. Preachers will want to note not only how the king reversed his decision, but also how Darius and Daniel both rose to power there as a result of the fall of Babylon, as described at the end of Daniel 5.

This detail is significant because the New Testament readings today focus on the reversal of powers in relation to another kingdom, the Roman Empire. In the book of Revelation, Babylon is a cryptic reference to Rome, and in chapter 18, an angel declares, "Fallen, fallen is Babylon the great!" (v 2). By announcing the fall of the Roman Empire, the angel gives hope to Christians who are oppressed by the state's unjust ways. Moreover, in Matthew 23, Jesus denounces the religious leaders of his day who are complicit in the Roman occupation of Jerusalem. Jesus is angry that, as puppets of the state, these leaders enjoy privileges that other people do not have, and he condemns them for their hypocrisy. Today's selection from the Gospel is the beginning of a longer reading that concludes on Lent 1 and serves as a thematic bridge between these seasons of repentance. Both New Testament texts today show how Jesus' coming overturns the oppressive powers of human empires.

While churches celebrate this Sunday before Christmas in different ways, today's readings about power reversals will leave lasting impressions on parishioners who are weary of how super-ficially many people observe Christmas at this time of year. Despite society's cries for saccharine sentimentality, today's readings are thematically consistent with the *RCL* texts for this day, which explicitly speak about the reversal of the world's powers (for example, Micah 5:2-5a in Year C or Luke 1:46b-55 in Years B or C). In Psalm 108 (a variant of Psalm 57, used in Advent 2), the author cries, "I will give thanks to you, O Lord, among the peoples, and I will sing praises to you among the nations" (v 3). When Jesus was born, the world's leaders and nations (such as Caesar in Rome) sought to glorify themselves. The birth of Jesus is a political statement that he, not the emperor, is the true Prince of Peace. In a day when empires and their leaders continue in self-serving ways, Advent reveals that Jesus is a different kind of leader in a realm which seeks the welfare of others and the praise of God.

Prayer: God, we pray that you would reverse the oppressive powers of human empires and liberate us to serve you in your realm of love and justice. Amen.

Christmas

Christmas Eve
Habakkuk 3:17-19
Isaiah 54:1-10
Philippians 4:10-14
Luke 2:1-20

On Christmas Eve, Christians celebrate a message of hope, proclaiming the birth of the Messiah as well as God's incarnation in the world. The readings offered here may be used for either Christmas Eve or Day, depending on local church tradition. As mentioned in the introduction, today's Gospel text is such an essential part of Christmas Eve celebrations that replacing it does not seem wise. Although Matthew 1:18-25 offers a birth narrative and John 1:1-14 speaks about the Word becoming flesh, these both appear on Sundays in the RCL and neither captures the fullness of the Christmas story as Luke 2:1-20 renders it. This passage eloquently relates the birth of Jesus, with angels and shepherds announcing this good news to a world that yearns to hear it.

The accompanying scriptures also speak a word of hope to people filled with despair. The reading from Habakkuk 3 offers an uplifting message for those facing times when life goes terribly wrong. "Though the fig tree does not blossom," the prophet says, "and no fruit is on the vines; though the produce of the olive fails and the fields yield no food; though the flock is cut off from the fold and there is no herd in the stalls, yet I will rejoice in the Lord; I will exult in the God of my salvation" (vv 17-18). Similarly, the passage from Isaiah 54 offers hope to an exiled people in despair. It specifically speaks to women who are barren or have been abandoned by their husbands. In a season in which birth is an important theme, this text can be a powerful pastoral witness to how God has compassion on us, even in times of high anxiety and loss. Finally, the text from Philippians 4 serves as a reminder that true joy and contentedness are not contingent on earthly circumstances. "I can do all things through him who strengthens me," (v 13) Paul writes. Because Christ's love is so deep and complete, people everywhere can face life's difficult situations with hope and courage.

Since Christmas celebrates more than the birth of a child, preachers may want to explore how they find hope in the teaching of the incarnation. They may wish to examine its intimate connection with the doctrine of resurrection, as today's readings could imaginatively serve as texts for either Christmas or Easter. While many people think that Christmas should be a happy time of year, it is often paradoxically a season of grief. Deaths, losses, or other causes for sadness often weigh heavily on people's hearts. In the midst of this grief, the words of these scriptures offer a message of hope for times when people feel despair. Preachers may also consider the significance of Philippians 4:14, in which Paul says, "In any case, it was kind of you to share in my distress." In the incarnation, God shares in people's distress by taking on all that it means to be human, thus providing hope amid the pain and suffering of life.

Prayer: Thank you, God, for coming to us and sharing in our joy and distress. Lift us up from our hopelessness and despair. We pray in the name of the child who is born to save and deliver us. Amen.

Christmas 1
Exodus 18:13-24
Psalm 69:30-36
1 Timothy 3:1-13
Matthew 1:1-17

Typically, Christmas 1 is the last Sunday in the calendar year and is often a day in which local churches have changes in leadership. New church officers are installed, while outgoing ones are thanked for their service. As the year transitions from old to new, today's readings from Exodus and 1 Timothy poignantly speak to the theme of leadership. In Exodus 18, Moses receives some good advice about delegating authority. His father-in-law, Jethro, admonishes him for trying to resolve all disputes and urges him to train leaders to share the work with him. 1 Timothy 3 outlines the responsibilities of the offices of bishop and deacon, providing an apt scriptural basis for the commissioning of new leaders. The selected verses from Psalm 69 offer praise to the God who leads all creation, a fitting theme in this Christmas season.

When readers consider the emphasis on leadership in these passages, today's Gospel reading may not initially seem to fit. Matthew 1 relates Jesus' genealogy, traced paternally through Joseph's line. While contemporary readers may not readily see it, these first seventeen verses may be the most carefully composed part of the whole book. Matthew is writing to a predominantly Jewish Christian audience, so he has a strong interest in showing how Jesus is rooted in Hebrew traditions. The symmetry between the generations as they are described in v 17 places an emphasis on order that would not be lost on the recipients of his work. Additionally, because some of the names listed in Jesus' lineage are figures of questionable character, they would doubtlessly raise a few eyebrows among Matthew's readers.

In terms of leadership, there is much to be gained by exploring the names in Matthew 1 and the narratives behind them. Casual readers may see only a list here, but preachers have an opportunity to show their hearers the generations of stories that it represents. They may connect this lineage with that of their congregations, marveling that Jesus knows their people's names and histories better than the people do themselves. For faith communities whose existence spans decades or centuries, the implications of this truth in terms of leadership are significant.

Because these organizations have been affected by multi-generational influences, leaders can bring healing and hope to their congregations by differentiating themselves from parishioners in ways that are caring and relatively non-anxious. Though some may consider today's texts "too boring" for congregational reading, preachers can give powerful leadership to churches by engaging these fascinating passages.

Prayer: God of our past, present and future, we praise you for coming to us and for being with us. Lead us, amid all the challenges of life, to be the people you long for us to be. Amen.

Christmas 2
Isaiah 57:14-19
Psalm 106:47-48
1 John 3:11-14a; 4:1-6
Luke 1:1-4

Christmas 2 serves as a transitional time between the season of Christmas (celebrating the incarnation) and the day of Epiphany (signifying God's revelation to all people). Because Christmas is twelve days, there are some years in which the season only has one Sunday. When there are two, lectionary preachers may choose between readings for Christmas 2 or Epiphany. Today's New Testament readings thematically align well with the Christmas season. In 1 John 3, the author exhorts his readers to love one another. In chapter 4, he calls them to discern truth from falsehood and encourages them to do so by saying, "For the one who is in you is greater than the one who is in the world" (v 4). Today's Gospel text also speaks of truth, as Luke begins the first chapter of his book by saying that he wrote it so his benefactor, Theophilus ("Lover of God"), might have an authentic account of the story of Jesus. He brilliantly succeeds in this task by authoring a book that many literary scholars believe to be one of the most beautiful writings ever penned by the human hand. The truth of the incarnation and of God's love for people comes through clearly in these Christmas readings.

The remaining texts also contain themes that are appropriate to Christmas but could also apply to Epiphany. In Psalm 106, the author writes, "Save us, O Lord our God, and gather us from the nations, that we may give thanks to your holy name and glory in your praise" (v 47). The psalmist cries to God for salvation and also looks for hope in Israel's exile among the nations. Isaiah 57 also offers a word of encouragement to a people in exile. "Peace, peace, to the far and the near, says the Lord; and I will heal them" (v 19). Such a message celebrates the Christmas themes of hope and peace as well as the Epiphany theme of the revelation of God to people in all nations.

On this day that serves as a bridge between two seasons, preachers have an opportunity to challenge parishioners to work with hope toward the future. In Isaiah 57, the prophet says, "Build up, build up, prepare the way, remove every obstruction from my people's way" (v 14). As a new calendar year dawns, preachers may challenge their congregations to think about what God is building in the life of the church today. Insofar as the church strives to be a community where people build each another up in love and truth, it lays a foundation of faithfulness that should help it to live out its mission in the future.

Prayer: God, help us to proclaim the truths of your incarnation and revelation to all people in this world. We pray that your presence will embolden us to move confidently into the future. Amen.

Epiphany

Epiphany
Proverbs 3:5-8
Isaiah 56:3-5
Acts 15:1-21
John 7:25-31

Epiphany celebrates the revelation of Jesus' identity as Christ (Messiah, or "anointed one") to the Gentiles (non-Jewish people). In the *RCL*, the Gospel reading in all three years is the account in Matthew 2 of the visit of the wise men. This story, which describes how Eastern visitors follow the light of a star to Jesus, shows that the truth about him is revealed to people far and wide. In today's Gospel selection from John 7, a crowd wonders whether Jesus is the Christ and asks, "When the Messiah comes, will he do more signs than this man has done?" The implied answer is that his signs point to the truth that he must be the anointed one. The author of Proverbs 3 writes, "Trust in the Lord with all your heart, and do not rely on your own insight" (v 5). On the day of Epiphany, as a new calendar year begins, Christians are called to trust that, in Jesus, God is revealed to the peoples of the earth.

The remaining scriptures explicitly show how Gentiles are included in God's plan of salvation. In Deuteronomy 23, the author states, "No one whose testicles are crushed or whose penis is cut off shall be admitted to the assembly of the Lord" (v 1). Again, the writer declares, "No Ammonite or Moabite shall be admitted to the assembly of the Lord" (v 3). Today's selection from Isaiah 56, however, reverses all of this. The prophet writes, "Do not let the foreigner joined to the Lord say, 'The Lord will surely separate me from his people;' and do not let the eunuch say, 'I am just a dry tree'" (v 3). The author makes it clear that eunuchs (castrated males) and foreigners are now welcome in the temple. Similarly, in Acts 15, the first Christian council meets in Jerusalem and decides to include Gentiles in the life of the church. Paul, Barnabas, and Peter all speak in favor of this, and James sums it up by concluding, "Therefore I have reached the decision that we should not trouble those Gentiles who are turning to God, but we should write to them to abstain only from things polluted by idols and from fornication and from whatever has been strangled and from blood" (vv 19-20). These readings reveal how the Christian church came to fully embrace the Epiphany message of welcoming all people into God's house.

Today's texts clearly reveal that those who were once excluded for reasons of nationality or sexual/gender identity are now included in the fellowship of faith. These readings demonstrate that even in Biblical times the Christian community was a "multiracial, multicultural church, open and accessible to all." Given this reality, preachers have an opportunity to show parishioners how these ancient texts speak powerfully today about the radically inclusive character of God.

Prayer: We praise you, God, for the ways in which you show us that Jesus is the Messiah. By breaking down barriers of exclusivity, you reveal how the whole world is welcome in your house. Help us to include one another in your ministry, as you have included us. Amen.

Baptism of Christ/Epiphany I
Genesis 3:1-7, 22-24
Isaiah 4:2-6
Acts 15:22-35
John 3:22-30

Because Epiphany 1 is traditionally observed as Baptism of Christ Sunday, today's texts contain themes pertaining to both Epiphany and baptism. This is evident in today's New Testament readings, beginning with the continuation of last week's story about the Jerusalem Council. This selection from Acts 15 contains a letter to Gentile believers announcing the Council's decision to welcome them. The reading advances the inclusive theme of Epiphany, while today's Gospel text focuses on the theme of baptism. Though the Gospel selections in the *RCL* for this Sunday typically center around stories of Jesus' baptism as they are recorded in the three Synoptic Gospels (Matthew 3:13-17, Mark 1:4-11, and Luke 3:15-17, 21-22), today's reading in John 3 is different in that it is not a story about Jesus' baptism (which does not directly appear in John) but about his baptizing activity. This is described in v 22, and the disciples of John the Baptist are curious about it. "Here he is," they say, "baptizing, and all are going to him" (v 26). John the Baptist uses this as an opportunity to testify, both to who he is and who Jesus is, in vv 27-30.

The Hebrew Bible readings for this day also relate to the subject of baptism. In all three years of Epiphany 1 in the *RCL*, the "song of the wild storm" in Psalm 29 provides a thematic link to the water of baptism. Today's reading from Isaiah 4 uses similar water imagery in speaking about washing the filth and cleansing the bloodstains from the people of Israel. Since baptism is traditionally understood as a washing that removes sin, today's divided selection from Genesis 3 becomes crucially significant for Baptism of Christ Sunday. This is a story about the first human beings, Adam and Eve. It begins when Eve meets a talking serpent who asks her if she may eat fruit from any tree in the garden, and she says that God told her and Adam that if they ate the fruit from the tree in the middle of the garden, they would die. The serpent tells her that they will not die but will become like God, knowing good and evil. Eve eats the fruit and gives some to Adam, who also eats it. They see they are naked and make clothing for themselves. God then expels Adam out of Eden to till the ground. This is the story that is referred to as "the fall," and baptism, as it is traditionally understood, serves as a cleansing from the "depravity" that results from the "original sin" of Adam and Eve's disobedience.

As preachers think about the connections between these readings and baptism, they may want to consider whether Genesis 3 was intended to be used as a doctrine universally condemning humankind to sin or whether it was written as a story attempting to explain why things are the way they are. Preachers should also be aware that if they use this occasion to celebrate the gift of baptism, they cannot assume that all their listeners have been baptized. They will want to consider how baptism might be presented as a sign of hope and life rather than insurance from the flames of a hell that the author of Genesis 3 never likely imagined.

Prayer: God, show us this day how to celebrate the gift of baptism. Amen.

Epiphany 2
Genesis 32:3-7a, 33:1-4
Psalm 44:23-26
Acts 5:33-42
John 8:12-20

Today's readings focus on how important grace is in helping people let go of their claims to exclusivity in their relationships with God. In John 8, Jesus declares, "I am the light of the world" (v 12). In this and other similar passages in John, Jesus is not intending to alienate twenty-first century people of different faiths, but he appeals to his followers to keep their focus on him. Such a focus is difficult to maintain in troubled times. The author of Psalm 44 cries, "Why do you sleep, O Lord? Awake, do not cast us off forever! Why do you hide your face? Why do you forget our affliction and oppression?" (vv 23-24). When people are anxious, they tend to lose sight of a gracious God and cling to self-justifying prejudices that belittle others.

Thankfully, today's remaining texts offer models of how God's grace empowers people to be gracious to others. Genesis 32 and 33 convey an important message, appropriate in these Sundays after Epiphany, about the role Gentiles play in God's plan of grace. Esau (who represents the Edomites) has reason to seek vengeance against his brother, Jacob (who represents the Israelites), because Jacob stole his birthright and blessing from their father, Isaac. Jacob expects that Esau will attack him, but when they meet, Esau instead shows him mercy. Such unanticipated mercy is an act of grace that is shown *by* Gentiles (in this case, the Edomites) *to* the Israelites, and its inclusion in the Hebrew Bible is an act of grace that is shown *by* the people of Israel *to* Gentiles. The final reading from Acts 5 describes an unexpected act of grace shown *by* Jewish leaders *to* the followers of Jesus. Again, its inclusion in the Christian canon is also an act of grace shown *by* Christians *to* the Jewish people. Gamaliel, a Pharisee and member of the council, convinces his colleagues to let a group of accused disciples of Jesus go free. "So in the present case, I tell you," he declares, "Let them alone; because if this plan or this undertaking is of human origin, it will fail; but if it of God, you will not be able to overthrow them - in that case you may even be found fighting against God" (vv 38-39).

These readings convey powerful messages on the theme of "letting go." While the Greek word "aphiemi" has different connotations depending on the context in which it is used, its primary meaning is "to let go." This is the sense in which Gamaliel uses the word when he tells the people to leave the disciples alone. The concept of "aphiemi" as mercy is a spiritual virtue of the highest order. In times when people are quick to take sides in present culture wars, the practice of letting go of exclusive claims to God's favor can be a humbling move that helps people avoid taking the wrong side and fighting against God. In a day when people are often quick to speak, slow to listen, and slower still to understand the positions of others, today's scriptures can be a healing pause that allows them to hear what their brothers and sisters who differ from them are really saying. In the process, they may discover ways of giving or receiving mercies that they might never otherwise have expected to encounter.

Prayer: God, show us mercy so that we may let go of claims to exclusivity and love our sisters and brothers as you call us to do. Amen.

Epiphany 3
Numbers 22:22-35; 23:7-12
Psalm 56:10-13
Acts 8:9-13, 18-25
Mark 4:21-23

Themes of light, grace, faithfulness and revelation to the Gentiles continue to show themselves in the readings for the Sundays after Epiphany. Today's selections from Psalm 56 and Mark 4 contain vivid images of light. The author of Psalm 56 declares, "For you have delivered my soul from death, and my feet from falling, so that I may walk before God in the light of life" (v 13). In Mark 4, Jesus states that lamps are not to be placed under bushel baskets. "For there is nothing hidden," he says, "except to be disclosed; nor is anything secret, except to come to light" (v 22). Such readings as these show how God continues to be revealed to people during this season.

God's inclusive message to the Gentiles is dramatically shown in the story of Simon the magician in Acts 8. He is amazing the (Gentile) Samaritans with his magic when Philip persuades him to be baptized. On witnessing the miracles the apostles are performing, he tries to buy the Holy Spirit from Peter, who rebukes him for thinking that God could be bought. By doing this, Peter teaches Simon that, unlike the economy of this world, God's good news is a gift on which no one can place a price. The story ends with Peter proclaiming this message of grace to villages of Samaritans.

Today's final selection from Numbers also conveys themes of grace and faithfulness by relating another entertaining tale about a failed attempt to buy God's favor. Preachers may want to set the stage for this story by describing how in Numbers 22:1-21, King Balak of Moab sends messengers to influence the prophet Balaam to curse Israel. Balaam at first resists by saying, "Although Balak were to give me his house full of silver and gold, I could not go beyond the command of the Lord my God, to do less or more" (v 18). Then, however, he succumbs and goes with them. This is where today's selection begins. In chapter 22, God is angry at Balaam's decision and sends an angel to stand in his way. Balaam does not see the angel, but his donkey does. The animal stops and is rewarded for its loyalty with a severe beating from its master. Then, the donkey starts to talk. "Am I not your donkey," the animal asks, "which you have ridden all your life to this day? Have I been in the habit of treating you this way?" (v 30). Balaam's silly responses incredulously offer no suggestion that there is anything unusual about donkeys talking to people. The angel comes to the animal's defense and, in doing so, teaches Balaam a lesson in loyalty. Balaam shows he has learned that lesson by blessing Israel as he does in Numbers 23. He has not allowed himself to be sold out by King Balak's influence after all. A changed Balaam now shows the kind of loyalty and obedience to God that a faithful donkey once showed to him.

Prayer: God, help us to be voices of blessing rather than cursing. Help us to be people who gladly receive your free gift of grace and are faithful to you. Amen.

Epiphany 4
Joshua 2:1-9, 12-16
Psalm 117
Acts 9:23-31
Mark 8:22-26

Today's readings continue to echo the Epiphany themes of light and revelation to the Gentiles and also address the power of God's deliverance. In Mark 8, Jesus puts saliva on the eyes of a blind man and lays hands on him. The man senses light and tells Jesus, "I can see people, but they look like trees, walking" (v 24). Jesus lays hands on him a second time, which allows the man to then see clearly. In Psalm 117, the psalmist writes, "Praise the Lord, all you nations! Extol him, all you peoples!" Both of these readings speak to God's self-revealing work to people everywhere.

Today's other texts show how Gentiles are included in God's saving work and emphatically offer readers a message of deliverance. In Joshua 2, a group of Israelite spies set out to determine whether their army can conquer the land of Canaan. As they enter the city of Jericho, they meet Rahab, a Canaanite (Gentile) prostitute, who hides them in her house. When they prepare to leave, she gives them instructions on how to avoid capture. Then, she drops a rope through her window and lowers them down to safety. The apostle Paul is similarly lowered to safety in today's reading from Acts 9. Chapter 9 begins when Saul, a persecutor of the church, travels the road to Damascus and encounters a blinding light. He hears Jesus' voice asking him, "Saul, Saul, why do you persecute me?" (v 4). After getting up, he enters the city and goes to the home of a man named Judas. There, a disciple called Ananias lays hands on him and restores his sight. With a new identity, Saul changes his name to Paul. He begins to preach in Damascus, and today's selection starts as violent opposition rises against him there. Aware of Paul's predicament, some disciples take him by night and lower him to safety through an opening in the city wall. After he is safe, he goes to Jerusalem and boldly engages the Hellenists (Gentiles) there. Disciples who were once afraid of him begin to believe in him, and the good news about Jesus spreads throughout the region. Both of these readings powerfully show how God is able to deliver people from life-threatening situations.

Preachers who focus on these last two texts can use them to demonstrate how God's deliverance of the Israelite spies and Paul (who are all lowered down walls to safety) leads to the liberation of Gentile people. Rahab's deliverance of the spies in Joshua 4 will eventually lead to her own freedom, as next Sunday's selection from Judges 6 will demonstrate. Also, Paul's deliverance from authorities in Acts 9 frees him to engage the Greeks in Jerusalem and begin a lifelong journey of ministry to Gentiles. As the Sundays after Epiphany progress, these texts continue to reveal God's amazing ability to include and save people far and wide.

Prayer: God of Israel, the nations, and the universe, we praise you for revealing yourself to us and setting us free to be your people. As you have delivered us from death, help us to welcome others into your ministry of liberation. Amen.

Epiphany 5
Joshua 6:1-5, 15-25
Psalm 135:1-7
Acts 10:1-28
Luke 11:34-36

As the Sundays after Epiphany progress, images of light, revelation and liberation remain prominent in the selected readings. The author of Psalm 135 praises God by saying, "He it is who makes the clouds rise at the end of the earth; he makes lightnings for the rain and brings out the wind from his store-houses" (v 7). Also on the subjects of light and revelation, Jesus, in Luke 11, declares, "Your eye is the lamp of your body. If your eye is healthy, your whole body is full of light; but if it is not healthy, your body is full of darkness" (v 34). Such texts as these illuminate the theme of revelation and accentuate the remaining passages' emphases on freedom.

As with last week's readings, today's selections from Joshua and Acts reveal liberating messages to faithful groups of Gentiles. Joshua 6, which follows up on last week's account of the deliverance of the spies, describes how Joshua leads the Israelites to march on Jericho. With a shout and the sound of trumpets, the city walls, in the words of a modern spiritual, come "a' tumbling down." Rahab, the Canaanite prostitute, is spared, along with her household. The Israelites have been true to their promise to this Gentile woman, who proves to be instrumental in delivering Jericho into Israel's hands. The story reveals the paradox that even though Gentiles are saved by God's liberating action they also have a critical role to play in God's wider plan of salvation. This truth is also revealed in the reading from Acts 10 in which an angel sends a Gentile centurion named Cornelius to search for Peter at the home of Simon the tanner. Prior to the soldier's arrival, Peter goes up on the roof of Simon's house and prays. There he has a vision of a giant sheet coming down from heaven. The sheet has all kinds of unclean animals in it, and he hears a voice commanding him to eat them. When he protests, the voice says, "What God has made clean, you must not call profane" (v 15). This happens three times, and the sheet is taken up into heaven. When Cornelius enters, Peter declares, "God has shown me that I should not call anyone profane or unclean" (v 28). In this way, Peter reveals the change of heart that God has given him concerning the inclusion of the Gentiles in the life of the church.

The liberating message found in the readings from Joshua 6 and Acts 10 is a compelling one for this season. The reception of

Gentiles in the early church makes a convincing case for the inclusion of marginalized people in the church today. With echoes of the story of tumbling Jericho walls fresh in parishioners' ears, preachers may powerfully speak about how God shatters walls of exclusivity with a sheet that falls from heaven. If God breaks down walls that exclude Gentiles in scripture, how might Christians today see God removing barriers before people who are marginalized in contemporary society?

Prayer: God, break down those walls that exclude us from one another and you. Amen.

Note: For the years when the liturgical calendar contains more than six Sundays after Epiphany, please turn ahead to Proper 1/Epiphany 6, Proper 2/Epiphany 7, and Proper 3/Epiphany 8.

Last Sunday after Epiphany/Transfiguration Sunday
Genesis 14:18-20
Psalm 110:1-4
Hebrews 7:1-3, 11-19
John 5:30-47

Transfiguration Sunday typically observes what many call the "ultimate Epiphany" of the Transfiguration story. This narrative, found only in the Synoptic Gospels, is well-utilized by the *RCL* in Matthew 17:1-9, Mark 9:2-9, and Luke 9:28-43. It relates how Peter, James and John see Jesus' face and clothes become radiant while Moses and Elijah appear with him. Though this story itself is absent in today's Gospel reading, John 5 is filled with imagery relating to the Transfiguration. Jesus speaks about such witnesses to his glory as John the Baptist, about whom he says, "He was a burning and shining lamp, and you were willing to rejoice for a while in his light. But I have a testimony greater than John's" (vv 35-36). Jesus claims not to accept glory from human beings, and he challenges his listeners by saying, "How can you believe when you accept glory from one another and do not seek the glory from the one who alone is God?" (v 44). He also appeals to Moses (a witness to Jesus' Transfiguration in the Synoptic accounts) by declaring, "If you believed Moses, you would believe me, for he wrote about me" (v 46). In all of these ways, John 5 testifies to Epiphany's climax as it is revealed in Jesus' glorification.

The remaining texts for this Sunday contain obvious thematic links between Jesus and a mysterious priest called Melchizedek. On a day when the "ultimate Epiphany" is celebrated, Melchizedek may be seen as the ultimate righteous Gentile to whom the revelation of God has come. This enigmatic figure first appears in Genesis 14, in which the author writes, "And King Melchizedek of Salem brought out bread and wine; he was a priest of God Most High" (v 18). After greeting Abram, Melchizedek blesses him. Melchizedek later appears in Psalm 110, as the psalmist tells an unnamed leader in Israel, "The Lord has sworn and will not change his mind, 'You are a priest forever according to the order of Melchizedek'" (v 4). Still later, in Hebrews 7, the New Testament author writes about the significance of Melchizedek for a Christian understanding of the Messiah's identity. "Without father, without mother, without genealogy, having neither beginning of days nor end of life, but resembling the Son of God, he remains a priest forever" (v 3). The author identifies Jesus as the "great high priest" of Christians who becomes a priest "not through a legal requirement concerning physical descent, but through the power of an indestructible life" (v 16). By connecting Jesus to the Gentile figure of Melchizedek, the author of Hebrews shows how God's glory in Jesus is revealed to all people.

Preachers have a tremendous opportunity with today's readings to show that Jesus' connection to an ancient Gentile priest testifies to the Epiphany theme of the inclusion of all people in God's plan of salvation. By using these texts, they will put an exclamation point on how this climactic final Sunday after

Epiphany proclaims a message of grace to people everywhere.

Prayer: God, on this Transfiguration Sunday, we pray that we might see anew how you include all people in the light of your glory and grace. Amen.

Lent

Ash Wednesday
Jeremiah 7:1-15
Isaiah 29:9-10, 13-16
James 1:12-16
Matthew 6:7-13

Lent is a season of repentance lasting forty days, not counting Sundays, and the number forty in Jewish tradition suggests a long period of time. It is a season of spiritual discipline that is often connected with acts of self-denial, self-examination, resistance to temptation, and devotion to righteousness. It invites us to follow Jesus through his Galilean ministry as he sets his face toward Jerusalem, suffers and dies. It begins with Ash Wednesday, which calls us to consider our mortality by reminding us that we are dust and to dust we will return. The scriptures for this day in the *RCL* are the same in years A, B, and C (Joel 2:1-2, 12-17 or Isaiah 58:1-12; Psalm 51:1-17; 2 Corinthians 5:20b-6:10; and Matthew 6:1-6, 16-21), and they focus in varying degrees on the disciplines of prayer, almsgiving, and fasting. In the liturgy for Ash Wednesday, worshipers are called to turn away from their sins and believe in the good news. Many churches observe this day by imposing ashes and/or celebrating Holy Communion. In the midst of these acts of worship, today's recommended readings are appropriate, yet challenging.

The first three readings amplify the themes of the season. Jeremiah 7 is a portion of the prophet's "Temple Sermon" in which he offers a message of judgment against those who trust in vain repetitions, false words and self-deceptive comforts. He offers a scathing indictment of their hypocrisy, calling for their words to match their deeds. "Amend your ways and your doings," Jeremiah declares, "and let me dwell with you in this place" (v 3). The tone of this passage closely resembles that of

Isaiah 29, a text of judgment that serves as a call to repentance. "You turn things upside down!" (v 16) the prophet cries. Like the *RCL*'s selections from the Hebrew Scriptures for this day, the divided reading in Isaiah 29 admonishes people to turn to God. In the New Testament, James 1 offers a word of blessing to anyone who practices the Lenten discipline of resisting temptation. "Such a one," the author says, "has stood the test and will receive the crown of life that the Lord has promised to those who love him" (v 12).

Perhaps the most compelling of these readings, however, is the text of the Lord's Prayer in Matthew 6. The *RCL*'s divided Gospel offering for Ash Wednesday (Matthew 6:1-6, 16-21) acts as two slices of bread in a textual "sandwich." The selection offered today (vv 7-13) provides the meat. While this reading is a variant of Luke 11:2-4, which appears in Proper 12 of Year C in the *RCL*, Matthew's version uses distinctive language about heaven (vv 9-10) and debts (v 12). It also includes petitions about God's will (v 10) and deliverance from evil (v 13). These variations make it different enough to stand on its own here, and preachers may be surprised to witness how people receive it when it is read as a portion of scripture instead of shared as a spoken prayer. As the season of spiritual discipline that is Lent begins, what better time could there be to explore the model prayer that Jesus offers?

Prayer: God, remind us that we are dust and to dust we shall return. Help us to turn away from our sins and believe in the good news. Amen.

Lent I
Amos 2:4-8, 13-16
Psalm 25:16-18
Galatians 5:2-12
Matthew 23:27-36

Lent is, among other things, a season of enduring tests, and these proposed readings compel Christians to examine ways in which the church has misused the Bible to keep certain people in states of oppression. As Lent begins, the Hebrew Bible selection presents the prophet Amos proclaiming judgment on Judah and Israel. There are no niceties in Amos 2, no mincing of words. The prophet's judgment comes on swiftly and hard. The same is true in Galatians 5, where Paul speaks against the "pro-circumcision" faction at that church in the harshest of terms. In his invective against them, he exclaims, "I wish those who unsettle you would castrate themselves!" (v 12). As one of Paul's early epistles, Galatians reveals more of Paul's impatience and irritability than some of his later, more developed letters.

In today's Gospel text, Jesus not only examines the scribes and Pharisees but judges them harshly. Today's selection from Matthew 23 concludes the Gospel passage that was introduced on the Fourth Sunday of Advent (vv 13-26). Preachers may note the link between these seasons, which not only share the liturgical color of violet but also the themes of preparation, self-examination, awakening and repentance.

Today's texts present a difficult challenge that compels not only preachers but the Christian community as a whole to practice self-examination. The fact that Jesus castigates Jewish leaders in Matthew 23 may lead readers to think that, despite his Jewish identity, he is taking a stand against Jews. This argument, which has exacerbated anti-Semitism among some, is based on faulty, noncritical interpretations of this passage. Much damage in the history of Jewish-Christian relations has been done by this type of thinking. Similarly, when Amos speaks words of judgment against a host of nations in chapters 1 and 2, his harshest rhetoric is aimed at Judah and Israel. This, too, has wrongly fueled flames of anti-Semitism among later readers of the prophet's words. In the case of Galatians 5, some say that Paul is being an "in-house" critic in his pronouncement against the "pro-circumcision" faction at that church. They maintain that he is not speaking against Jews but against those who insist that one must undergo certain rituals (rooted in Judaism) to receive the salvation that Paul believes to be a gift of grace. Others, though, hold that despite this, Paul's rhetoric advances anti-Semitic themes. For these reasons, today's texts are tremendously challenging for twenty-first century preachers. When recalling the Holocaust, as well as centuries of pogroms against Jews, Christians must consider how Biblical rhetoric has been misinterpreted to wrongly fuel bigotry and hatred. In today's reading from Psalm 25, the psalmist prays, "Consider my affliction and my trouble, and forgive all my sins" (v 18). As people who have received forgiveness, Christians are called to preach a message of love in the world, not hate.

Prayer: God, forgive us for wrongly using the Bible to justify hatred and violence against our Jewish brothers and sisters. Have mercy on us and change us. Amen.

Lent 2
Genesis 9:18-27
Psalm 39:4-8a
Titus 2:1-10
Matthew 12:38-42

The readings in this season continue to lift up a variety of Lenten themes. Psalm 39 contains a reflection on mortality and a call for deliverance from transgressions. In Matthew 12, Jesus responds to those who seek confirmation of his ministry by offering "the sign of the prophet Jonah" (v 39). "For just as Jonah was three days and three nights in the belly of the sea monster," he says, "so for three days and three nights the Son of Man will be in the heart of the earth" (v 40). This reference to Jesus' suffering and death is focal to Christians' Lenten journeys to the cross and tomb.

The remaining readings for this day focus on ways in which God calls Christians to repent of misusing the Bible to the unjust exclusion and oppression of others. In Genesis 9, Ham sees his father, Noah, lying naked and drunk in his tent. In that culture, seeing one's father naked would have been shameful. Ham tells his brothers, Shem and Japheth, what he has seen, and his brothers walk backward into the tent to cover up their father. When Noah becomes sober, he declares, "May God make space for Japheth, and let him live in the tents of Shem; and let Canaan be his slave" (v 27). The rhetorical point of the story is to implicate Israel's enemies, the Canaanites, as being shameful from their very beginning. Over the course of history, however, Jewish, Christian and Muslim leaders developed the teaching that Canaan was actually a dark skinned African. With this false interpretation, they justified enslaving African peoples. Those seeking further Biblical validation of slavery turned to the "household code" in Titus 2. Such codes in the New Testament (for example, Ephesians 5:21-6:9 or Colossians 3:18-4:1) are concerned with order and structure in family life. Authoritarian and patriarchal in nature, they conclude with exhortations concerning slaves. The author of Titus tells slaves to be "submissive to their masters and to give satisfaction in every respect; they are not to talk back, not to pilfer, but to show complete and perfect fidelity" (vv 9-10). Such justifications for slavery fed the racist subjugation of African people in Europe and the Americas for centuries.

The fact that at the time of this writing a man of African

American heritage is President of the United States may lead some to think that the struggle for racial justice in the world is complete. Nothing could be further from the truth. The legacy of African enslavement has scarred humanity so deeply that the world is still far from being a racially just place. Some Christians observe one Sunday in Lent as Amistad Sunday. This commemorates the 1839 uprising of Mendi slaves against their European captors aboard the schooner, La Amistad. As Christians then worked to set the accused Africans free, preachers today are also called to proclaim a message of liberation from the horrific legacies of slavery and racism. In doing so, they will need to imaginatively reconstruct the Biblical household codes to show that order and harmony need not be, and are best not, accompanied by patriarchy, racism, subjugation and fear.

Prayer: Have mercy on us, God, for ways in which we have abused power to oppress others by racism. Help us to turn from our sins so we might live in a just world. Amen.

Lent 3
Judges 11:29-40
Psalm 57:1-3
1 Timothy 2:11-15
Luke 19:41-44

These readings continue to advance the Lenten theme of penitent sorrow by Christians for misusing the Bible to oppress others. The author of Psalm 57 humbly pleads, "Be merciful to me, O God, be merciful to me, for in you my soul takes refuge; in the shadow of your wings I will take refuge, until the destroying storms pass by. I cry to God Most High, to God who fulfills his purpose for me" (vv 1-2). Jesus also cries out when he weeps for the future of Jerusalem in Luke 19. He says, "Indeed, the days will come upon you, when your enemies will set up ramparts around you and surround you, and hem you in on every side.

They will crush you to the ground, you and your children within you, and they will not leave within you one stone upon another; because you did not recognize the time of your visitation" (vv 43-44). Luke likely shares this incident not merely to evoke sorrow among his readers, but also to instill in them a desire to repent.

The selections from 1 Timothy 2 and Judges 11 are two tremendously difficult "texts of terror" that have wrongly been used to justify violence and oppression against women. The author of 1 Timothy 2 dismisses women's voices by saying, "Let a woman learn in silence with full submission" (v 11). Childless people today may be shocked to hear that women "will be saved through childbearing, provided they continue in faith and love and holiness, with modesty" (v 15). This passage will likely generate much hurt and anger among present day parishioners, as will today's Hebrew Bible selection. Judges 11 relates the horrific story of the warrior Jephthah, who comes home from battle and makes a vow to God, saying, "If you will give the Ammonites into my hand, then whoever comes out of the doors of my house to meet me, when I return victorious from the Ammonites, shall be the Lord's, to be offered up by me as a burnt offering" (v 31). After taking this oath, his only daughter runs out of the house to greet him, and he tells her about his promise. Astonishingly, she says, "Do to me according to what has gone out of your mouth" (v 36), asking only for a couple of months' reprieve. The emphasis placed on her virginity has led some to believe that this incident does not deal with human sacrifice but with Jephthah's refusal to allow her to be married. The story's conclusion, however, tragically suggests otherwise.

The readings from 1 Timothy 2 and Judges 11 present enormous preaching difficulties. They are part of the "unconscious content" of scripture that most preachers would rather (and often do) ignore. While trying to address them in terms of their cultural context may help parishioners understand them better, the damage these passages have done to women over the centuries is impossible to excuse. As women around the world continue to experience abuse at the hands of violent men, preachers should consider how to confront and even oppose these texts in order to offer a word of hope, especially to abused women who are listening to their sermon.

Prayer: God, have mercy on us for the abuse committed against women, and forgive our attempts to justify such violence on the basis of scripture. Change us, we pray. Amen.

Lent 4
Leviticus 18:19-22; 19:19, 27-28
Psalm 118:5-9
Romans 1:18-2:11
Mark 10:32-34

As we progress through our Lenten pilgrimage, we continue to examine how Christians have misused scripture in order to keep others marginalized. Today's brief reading from Mark 10 addresses the pilgrimage motif by describing Jesus' journey to Jerusalem, during which he tells them about his impending death and resurrection. Meanwhile, the Hebrew Bible selection expounds on the theme of marginalization that appears throughout the texts in this season. These verses in Leviticus 18 and 19 contain a variety of prohibitions that appear to include a number of sexual issues (18:19, 20 and 22), child sacrifice to Molech (18:21), breeding different kinds of animals, sowing different kinds of seed in a field, making a garment of various materials (19:19), rounding the hair of one's temples, marring beards (19:27), and tattoos (19:28). These prohibitions will seem strange to most readers today, especially when those with anti-gay agendas selectively emphasize Leviticus 18:22 and ignore surrounding verses.

Similarly, today's recommended text from Romans is one that

is often used against gay and lesbian people. While it is long, it is worth reading as a whole since Romans 2:1-11 sets in context what Paul says in 1:18-32. In chapter 1, Paul excoriates a group of idolatrous people when he says, "Full of envy, murder, strife, deceit, craftiness, they are gossips, slanderers, God-haters, insolent, haughty, boastful, inventors of evil, rebellious toward parents, foolish, faithless, heartless, ruthless" (vv 29-31). This description does not match that of most gay or lesbian people, who are often the antitheses of those epithets. Also, Paul's words on what is natural or unnatural in vv 26-27 reflect the cultural biases of his day and should be revisited in the light of current studies on gender and sexuality. Even a strained, literalistic reading of these verses, however, cannot obscure the fact that the purpose of Romans 1 is to direct readers to the greater point that Paul makes in Romans 2:1 where he says, "Therefore, you have no excuse, whoever you are, when you judge others; for in passing judgment on another you condemn yourself, because you, the judge, are doing the very same things." Paul's aim, then, is not to judge people on the basis of their sexual orientation, but for his whole audience to recognize its collective guilt and sin so they do not, as he puts it in chapter 2, "despise the riches of [God's] kindness and forbearance and patience" (v 4).

Today's readings from Leviticus and Romans are two of the principal texts that are used to exclude and condemn gays and lesbians. By situating these passages in their broader contexts, people may better understand the intentions of their authors and more faithfully reinterpret them today. The author of Psalm 118 writes, "The Lord is on my side to help me; I shall look in triumph on those who hate me" (v 7). By revealing the faulty logic of those who misuse these texts as weapons of hatred, preachers have a wonderful opportunity to show lesbian and gay people and their allies how God is indeed on their side to help them.

Prayer: God, forgive us for ways in which we have used the Bible to exclude gay and lesbian people. Help us to turn from our sins to work for justice in our time. Amen.

Lent 5
Deuteronomy 7:1-5
Psalm 141:1-4
Romans 13:1-7
Mark 13:21-23

On this final Sunday in Lent before Holy Week, preachers of the readings in *Beyond the Lectionary* mark an important point in their journey in which they have wrestled with ways that Christians have misused the Bible to oppress others. The difficulty of this point is emphasized in the deeply problematic reading they face from the Hebrew Bible today. The selected verses in Deuteronomy 7 are words of genocide and present a side of the Bible that most people of religious faith would rather not see. Referring to a number of nations in the area of Canaan, the author writes, "And when the Lord your God gives them over to you and you defeat them, then you must utterly destroy them. Make no covenant with them and show them no mercy" (v 2). Such violent and extreme emphases on ethnic, national and religious purity raise issues that are deeply troubling to Biblical interpreters today.

Another difficult passage that has been used to oppress others is found in Romans 13, where Paul says, "Let every person be subject to the governing authorities; for there is no authority except from God, and those authorities that exist have been instituted by God" (v 1). His seemingly unconditional defense of the state in this chapter leaves him open to the accusation that because he believes that God institutes government, civil disobedience must always be wrong. This may sound strange, especially given the persecuted status of many first century

Christians, including Paul, who was frequently imprisoned. It especially sounds strange given twenty-first century people's awareness of how governments throughout history committed horrific crimes against their own people. Tragically, such abuse continues to this day, and Christians must bristle at the thought that scripture could be used to sanction it.

This final Sunday before Holy Week reveals perhaps the most egregious sin that Christians have misused the Bible to justify. Namely, they have used scripture as a weapon to prove that they are right while others are wrong. Through the centuries, Christians have justified violence against their opponents, even though this is antithetical to the ministry of Jesus. Sadly, this sense of rightness has all too often become an idol, or false messiah, for Christians. In Mark 13 (which preachers may link to the Gospel text for Advent 3), Jesus says, "False messiahs and false prophets will appear and produce signs and omens, to lead astray, if possible, the elect. But be alert, I have already told you everything" (vv 22-23). Also, in the midst of trying times, the author of Psalm 141 prays, "I call upon you, O Lord; come quickly to me" (v 1a). As Christians draw near to Jerusalem in their Lenten journey with Jesus, these texts are a final reminder of the human need to call on God and repent of how people have wrongly used Biblical texts for evil instead of good.

Prayer: God of all nations and peoples, forgive us for being self-assured in our own rightness. Grant us humility, have mercy on us and help us to change. Amen.

Palm Sunday/Passion Sunday
Deuteronomy 16:1-3
Psalm 103:15-18
1 John 2:7-11, 15-17
John 16:16-33

Having experienced five Sundays of readings that are focused on repentance, the season now moves to the day when Christians observe Jesus' entry into Jerusalem and/or his Passion. The Passion stories in Matthew, Mark and Luke are covered over the RCL's three year cycle on this Sunday, and John's narrative is used each Good Friday. Because the RCL uses such a broad scope of readings this time of year, finding appropriate texts that it ignores is challenging. Today's first three readings, however, are just the kind of texts that set the stage for Holy Week. First, the selection from Deuteronomy 16 describes the Passover feast, the Jewish celebration that Jesus links with his own suffering and death. Those who fail to connect the events of Holy Week with this story miss much of the symbolism behind Christ's Passion. Psalm 103 then offers a preview of the Passion event by reflecting on human mortality and the love of God. This message of love continues in today's Epistle reading. 1 John as a whole eloquently emphasizes God's love, and the selected verses in chapter 2 speak about this love in the context of a new commandment. These readings serve as a prelude to Maundy Thursday, when Jesus shares the Passover meal with his disciples and commands them to love one another (John 13:34).

While all of these texts provide substantive material for preaching, today's Gospel reading beautifully shares what Jesus wants his disciples to know in the face of his impending death. In John 16, Jesus declares, "You will have pain, but your pain will turn into joy" (v 20). "So you have pain now; but I will see you again, and your hearts will rejoice, and no one will take your joy from you" (v 22). Again, he says, "I am not alone because the

Father is with me. I have said this to you, so that in me you may have peace. In the world you face persecution. But take courage; I have conquered the world!" (vv 32-33). Because this passage speaks a word of hope to the communal sense of grief, pain and loss that Christians experience this time of year, in some ways it communicates the story of Christ's Passion even more effectively than the traditional Gospel narratives.

Emotionally, psychologically, spiritually and physically, Christians move quickly from the stories of the cross to the grave to the empty tomb. In the process, they unavoidably experience grief, a product of hurt and anger over loss. Helping people work through grief, on individual and communal levels, takes time and is an essential part of ministry. Parishioners come to this time of year with their own wounds and anxieties. Having just been through a season in which they mourned the church's misuse of scripture, they now face the painful story of the cross and grave. Today's readings offer opportunities for individuals and communities to really wrestle with totality of their grief and work through it together as people of faith.

Prayer: O God revealed to us in Jesus, as you enter Jerusalem to suffer the cross and grave, teach us how to work through our grief and discover healing in your good news. Amen.

Maundy Thursday
Exodus 11:1-6; 12:29-36
Psalm 69:19-21
1 Corinthians 11:17-22, 27-34
John 15:18-25

Beyond the Lectionary includes readings for Maundy Thursday but not for Good Friday or Holy Saturday. There are a number of reasons for this, one of which is the aforementioned broad net that the *RCL* casts over relevant texts at this time of year. Another is the fact that different faith communities offer a variety of worship experiences during Holy Week. Some hold ecumenical or denominational community services on Good Friday and/or Holy Saturday. Others do not offer these, and still others combine them with Tenebrae services. Often when such worship services are offered, certain scriptures prevail. In the case of Good Friday, it may be the seven words from the cross or the Passion story in John 18 and 19. In the case of Holy Saturday, it may be the Great Vigil of Easter as prescribed in either the *RCL* or denominational worship books. Maundy Thursday, however, is widely observed as an important day of worship in Christian congregations and requires the kind of relevant scriptures offered here.

Today's readings speak to the Passion story, which the Last Supper liturgically enacts. The divided text from Exodus is a summary of the Passover and is vital for discerning meanings behind the events of Maundy Thursday and the Passion. For instance, if Jesus is the scapegoat whose death ends all cycles of blame and violence, then he acts here as the Passover lamb whose blood liberates people from death. Psalm 69 is also linked to the Passion story thematically, not only in terms of the author's cry, "Insults have broken my heart" (v 20), but also in terms of the vinegar in v 21 alluded to in Matthew 27:34 and John 19:29. John 15 speaks of the world's hatred and future persecutions of Jesus' followers. By saying, "They hated me without a cause," (v 25) Jesus implies that he is innocent as he becomes the scapegoat of and for the people.

While all of the texts fit the theme of the day, the selection from 1 Corinthians 11 may be the most engaging. The Epistle reading for this day in all three years of the *RCL* is vv 23-26, and today's divided reading contains some important words that precede and follow this passage. Verses 17-22 and 27-34 reveal much about Paul's concern for the ways that the Corinthians observed Holy Communion. Just as first century Christians heatedly debated differences in celebrating Communion, so do churches today. While the amount of food consumed by communicants may not be currently pressing, concerns about children receiving Communion, ways in which the sacrament is administered, and the frequency of celebrations are among the challenges facing today's church. Sadly, the anger that is generated over such disputes about Communion leads to the very kind of blaming and scapegoating that Jesus' death is supposed to end. When Paul talks about "discerning the body" (v 29), he is not talking about understanding everything that happens in Communion. Instead, he is calling the Corinthians to be mindful of their brothers and sisters who are sharing the meal with them. Maybe if Christians "discerned the body" in this way, many of the disputes that challenge the church today would disappear.

Prayer: God, we gather this night, when shadows have fallen, to share the gift of your self-giving love in Holy Communion. Help us to discern your presence among us. Amen.

Easter

Easter Sunday
2 Kings 4:18-20, 32-37
Isaiah 52:1-2
Acts 13:26-31
Mark 16:9-20

"Alleluia! Christ is risen! Christ is risen indeed! Alleluia!" The Easter proclamation of joy rings loud and clear through today's readings. The author of Isaiah 52 proclaims a message of freedom and deliverance by crying, "Shake yourself from the dust, rise up, O captive Jerusalem; loose the bonds from your neck, O captive daughter Zion!" (v 2). The text from Acts 13 serves as a synopsis of Christ's ministry, suffering, death, and resurrection, as Paul addresses the synagogue in Antioch of Pisidia. This reading is similar to Acts 10:34-43, which is prescribed on Easter Sunday in years A, B, and C of the *RCL*. The divided passage selected from 2 Kings 4 is an extraordinary text about Elisha raising the child of the Shunammite woman. One of the most profound passages in the Hebrew Bible on the subject of resurrection, it powerfully shows how God raises people not only from physical death, but also from the deaths of enslavement, infertility, illness and starvation.

Today's Gospel reading is also a challenging but significant resurrection story. It is probably denied inclusion on a Sunday in the *RCL* because of scholarly doubts about its originality. Most scholars dismiss both the longer and shorter endings of Mark as later additions to the text, and therefore, the *RCL* terminates its reading of Mark 16 at verse 8. The longer ending of Mark is included in its entirety here because even though it may be a later addition, it contains poignant messages about the resurrection that have been shared over centuries of Christian preaching. There is controversial material here, as when Jesus

49

states, "And these signs will accompany those who believe: by using my name they will cast out demons; they will speak in new tongues; they will pick up snakes in their hands, and if they drink any deadly thing, it will not hurt them they will lay their hands on the sick and they will recover" (vv 17-18). The point of these verses is not to put God to the test by recklessly endangering lives but to encourage people to have faith in Jesus and in the power of his resurrection. Christ's commission in this reading is powerful, as he commands his disciples, "Go into all the world and proclaim the good news to the whole creation" (v 15).

Preachers who are skeptical of how these readings might work on "high holy days" may be surprised by how well hearers receive these fresh texts on Easter Sunday. While the controversial material in the Gospel may be worth engaging as a preaching "hook," the commission to "Go" in v 15 contains within it the makings of memorable Easter sermons. Having completed the difficult journey of Lent, preachers are encouraged to embrace the freedom they find in these texts as well as the other scriptures that await them in this Easter season.

Prayer: God of resurrection, we praise you for raising us from the dust of death. Deliver us, we pray, from the powers of sin, evil and death, so that we might share in the glory of the life you promise us through the resurrection of Jesus, our Savior. Amen.

Easter 2
Exodus 5:22-6:13; 7:1-6
Psalm 18:1-6
Acts 3:1-10
Matthew 28:11-15

In this Easter season which celebrates how Jesus' resurrection sets people free from evil, sin and death, the scriptures offered here proclaim a message of deliverance. In today's divided selection from Exodus, Moses is called by God to liberate the Israelites from the oppressive, enslaving hand of the Egyptians. Moses and Aaron hear God's call and promise, and they respond obediently. The reading from Psalm 18 is also one of liberation. "The cords of death encompassed me," the psalmist writes. "The torrents of perdition assailed me; the cords of Sheol entangled me; the snares of death confronted me. In my distress I called to the Lord; to my God I cried for help. From his temple he heard my voice, and my cry to him reached his ears" (vv 4-6). Both of these readings testify to the delivering power of God.

This message of deliverance is also proclaimed in today's New Testament texts. Matthew 28 relates how the chief priests respond to the soldiers' message about Jesus' resurrection. Matthew writes, "After the priests had assembled with the elders, they devised a plan to give a large sum of money to the soldiers, telling them, 'You must say, "His disciples came by night and stole him away while we were asleep"'" (vv 12-13). The author shares these details in order to debunk rumors that Jesus' disciples stole his body and staged his resurrection. The story reveals that the soldiers are imprisoned by their greed and lies while the disciples are set free by their witness to the empty tomb. The other New Testament reading in Acts 3 tells the tale of a man who is unable to walk. He lies down by the Beautiful Gate and begs for help every day. Peter and John see him, and Peter says, "I have no silver or gold, but what I have I give you; in the name of Jesus Christ of Nazareth, stand up and walk" (v 6). The man leaps up freely and goes with them, and those who see this healing and liberating work are astonished.

Although today's texts celebrate God's deliverance in the victory of the resurrection, preachers will want to avoid a tone of triumphalism, especially in connection with the reading from Acts 3. People with physical disabilities or those who are trapped in poverty might find the story of the healing of the man who begs at the gate to be problematic. Why are some people healed from physical ailments when others are not? Why do some discover economic freedom while others are trapped in vicious circles of dependence? The Gospel message of liberation and new life is real and powerful, but preachers will want to explore this truth deeply instead of being content with a shallow message of earthly prosperity. By doing this, preachers will tap into a spiritual reality that liberates people in dynamic and healing ways.

Prayer: We praise you, God, for setting us free from every power that would imprison us. Help us to see that the freedom you give us is above and beyond any of the circumstances that we face in this life. Amen.

Easter 3
1 Samuel 20:12-23, 35-42
Psalm 18:46-50
Acts 4:13-22
John 21:20-25

Today's texts serve as powerful testimonies to the new life God gives in this Easter season. Psalm 18 describes how God delivers the author from enemies. The psalmist praises God, declaring, "For this I will extol you, O Lord, among the nations, and sing praises to your name" (v 49). The divided reading from 1 Samuel 20 offers further testimony to the gift of new life. Jonathan and David are dear friends who love each other, but Jonathan's father, King Saul, is threatened by David. Jonathan agrees to alert David with a signal if he thinks David's life is in danger. When Jonathan learns that his father plans to kill David, he goes out into the field and shoots arrows beyond a servant boy, who retrieves them. David understands the signal, and after Jonathan sends the boy away, the two men kiss each other and weep as they agree to part.

Jonathan tells David, "Go in peace, since both of us have sworn in the name of the Lord, saying, 'The Lord shall be between me and you, and between my descendants and your descendants forever'" (v 42). Even though their parting is painful, Jonathan's message saves David's life and testifies to the truth that even out of pain and suffering, God gives new life.

The New Testament readings further testify to the new life God gives, as they bear witness to Jesus and praise him. In John 21, Peter learns that Jesus' "beloved disciple" (traditionally understood to be the writer, John) may not suffer a martyr's death. In the final verse of the book, the author gives one more testimony to the works of Jesus, saying, "But there are also many other things that Jesus did; if every one of them were written down, I suppose that the world itself could not contain the books that would be written" (v 25). Also, in the reading from Acts 4, the rulers, elders, scribes and priests assemble for an inquiry concerning the man at the Beautiful Gate (from last week's reading in Acts 3), whom Peter and John healed in the name of Jesus. After debating the matter, they charge the disciples not to speak or teach any more in Jesus' name. Peter and John, however, respond by saying, "Whether it is right in God's sight to listen to you rather than to God, you must judge; for we cannot keep from speaking about what we have seen and heard" (vv 19-20). The disciples continue to witness to Jesus and praise him.

These selected verses from Acts 4, along with today's other readings, give preachers ample material to witness to the new life Jesus gives to people. They also show that a fitting response to such liberation and deliverance is one of praise. Parishioners who are facing intimidating situations will be emboldened by listening to the testimony given by Peter and John. They will be encouraged to hear that open testimonies to the truth triumph over deceptive conspiracies of silence. In this season of Easter, such themes of proclamation and praise will be welcomed by those who know that God has given them new life and are not afraid to share it.

Prayer: We praise you, God, for delivering us from death to new life. Empower us, so that we may be bold in testifying to your saving work in the world. Amen.

Easter 4

Ezekiel 34:25-31
Psalm 28
1 Timothy 4:6-16
Luke 15:4-10

The liturgical calendar observes Easter 4 as Good Shepherd Sunday. On this day, texts are tailored toward shepherding imagery, as Christians reflect on God's activity in gathering, protecting, nurturing and leading. The author of Psalm 28 pleads with God on behalf of Israel, saying, "O save your people, and bless your heritage; be their shepherd and carry them forever" (v 9). The prophet Ezekiel distinguishes between Israel's false shepherds, and God, their true shepherd. In Ezekiel 34, God promises to make a covenant of peace with the people. Through this covenant, Israel will find security from the false leaders in the land. "You are my sheep," God says to them, "the sheep of my pasture and I am your God, says the Lord God" (v 31). Also, in today's reading from Luke 15, Jesus asks, "Which one of you, having a hundred sheep and losing one of them, does not leave the ninety-nine in the wilderness and go after the one that is lost until he finds it?" (v 4). He speaks about the joy of the one who finds the lost sheep and compares that feeling to the joy that fills heaven when a sinner repents. He then tells a parallel story comparing the joy of a woman who finds a lost coin to that of heaven when a sinner turns to God. All of these scriptures use sheep and shepherding imagery to show how God leads people in this Easter season.

Shepherds, by definition, are leaders, and leadership is a key theme in 1 Timothy 4. In this text, the author admonishes Timothy, "If you put these instructions before the brothers and sisters, you will be a good servant of Christ Jesus, nourished on the words of the faith and of the sound teaching that you have followed" (v 6). He offers this young leader in the church practical advice on the kind of leadership that is essential for pastoral ministry. "Let no one despise your youth," he says, "but set the believers an example in speech and conduct, in love, in faith, in purity" (v 12). The author reminds Timothy of his commissioning to ministry when he declares, "Do not neglect the gift that is in you, which was given to you through prophecy with the laying on of hands by the council of elders" (v 14). He exhorts him further by saying, "Pay close attention to yourself and to your teaching; continue in these things, for in doing this you will save both yourself and your hearers" (v 16). This call to self-examination, courage, clarity, and humility offers a great challenge to pastors and church leaders today.

The metaphor of shepherding for leadership is a powerful one, and preachers must be attentive that they do not misuse these texts for self-aggrandizing purposes. Pastors are probably better viewed as "sheepdogs" than shepherds. Sheepdogs, like sheep, are accountable to the shepherd. While this metaphor goes only so far, it serves to remind pastors and parishioners alike that God is the Good Shepherd of all people.

Prayer: Remind us, God, that you are our Good Shepherd. We pray that those of us who lead in the church will do so by following you. Amen.

Easter 5
2 Samuel 9:1-13a
Psalm 68:17-20
Revelation 19:1-10
Mark 8:1-10

While themes of feasting fill the texts for today, the Hebrew Bible readings also proclaim a message of deliverance. In Psalm 68, the author declares, "Our God is a God of salvation, and to God, the Lord, belongs escape from death" (v 20). Such deliverance is also witnessed in the story of David's compassion to Mephibosheth in 2 Samuel 9. Having defeated Saul, David wants to show kindness to someone in Saul's house. Saul's servant Ziba tells David about Jonathan's son Mephibosheth who is "crippled in his feet" (v 3). The story of this injury is chronicled in 2 Samuel 4:4, which in part reads, "He [Mephibosheth] was five years old when the news about Saul and Jonathan came from Jezreel. His nurse picked him up and fled; and, in her haste to flee, it happened that he fell and became lame." Upon learning about Mephibosheth, David sends for him and tells him, "I will restore to you all the land of your grandfather Saul, and you yourself shall eat at my table always" (v 7). Mephibosheth, being aware of how poorly his grandfather treated David, protests, "What is your servant, that you should look upon a dead dog such as I?" (v 8). David, however, remains true to his word by delivering Mephibosheth from an otherwise uncertain fate and welcoming him to his table.

The New Testament selections offered here also advance the Easter themes of deliverance and feasting. The selection from Mark 8 relates the story of the feeding of the four thousand, which is also found in Matthew 15:32-39. Some scholars consider the feeding of the four thousand to be a variant of the feeding of the five thousand, but the fact that Matthew and Mark include both stories in their books indicates that the Biblical editors considered them to be separate and distinct accounts. Feeding miracles such as these in the Gospels typically represent Eucharistic experiences and offer glimpses of the heavenly banquet shared by God's people. Such a banquet is also celebrated in Revelation 19. In this passage, an angel exults, "Blessed are those who are invited to the marriage supper of the Lamb" (v 9). This wedding feast occurs after the destruction of evil powers, and a victorious multitude gathers to worship and praise God. The climactic songs of those assembled proclaim the Easter message of God's triumph over the powers of sin, evil and death.

Preachers cannot escape the twin themes of deliverance and feasting which abound in today's readings. On Easter Sunday, families may have gathered around tables to feast, and in this season Christians continue to celebrate the ongoing good news of how God delivers people from sin, evil and death. In these holy days, God sustains spiritually hungry people with the life giving message that through Jesus' resurrection, they are saved and delivered from every evil circumstance and even from death itself.

Prayer: God, deliver us from every evil that would keep us from you. Feed us with your bread and receive us at your table. Amen.

Easter 6
1 Kings 17:1-6
Psalm 134
Revelation 20:11-14a
John 4:46-54

Today's scriptures proclaim a message of life in the face of death, as God continues to deliver people from dire situations. An example of this is the story of God's provision for the prophet Elijah in 1 Kings 17. After Elijah declares that there will be a famine in the land, he goes and hides by the Wadi Cherith (Cherith Brook). God commands him to drink from the brook and tells him that ravens will bring him food. In the morning and evening, the birds come and deliver him life-sustaining bread and meat. Similarly, in John 4, Jesus comes to visit an official's son who is ill to the point of death. Jesus tells him that his son will live, and the boy is healed. After this, the official and his whole household believe in Jesus. In both instances, God intervenes in people's lives to deliver them from certain death to new life.

While the aforementioned scriptures speak about God delivering people from starvation and critical illness, today's selection from Revelation 20 shows how God saves people from death on a cosmic level. John of Patmos relates his vision when he writes, "And the sea gave up the dead that were in it, Death and Hades gave up the dead that were in them, and all were judged according to what they had done. Then Death and Hades were thrown into the lake of fire" (vv 13-14). The proclamation that this reading makes about the end of death announces a new life for people that is universal in scope.

These texts are fitting for the Easter season since they proclaim a message of how God delivers people from death to new life. Preachers will find abundant material in today's selections to show that God rescues people from famine, disease and even death itself. An appropriate response to such a message of deliverance may be found in Psalm 134, in which the author writes, "Lift up your hands to the holy place, and bless the Lord" (v 2). As God continues to bless people with the gift of new life in this season, preachers will do well to respond to the good news of God's victory over death with words of praise and thanksgiving.

Prayer: Thank you, God, for delivering us from evil, sickness and death. We praise you for blessing us, and our whole universe, with the gift of the new life that we witness in our risen Savior, Jesus. Amen.

Easter 7/Ascension Sunday
Jeremiah 38:1-13
Psalm 142
Revelation 21:15-21
John 7:32-36

Christians observe Jesus' ascension into heaven on the fortieth day of the Easter season. Because this event falls on a Thursday, churches have the option to celebrate it on the following Sunday, Easter 7. Because the principal texts describing Jesus' ascension (Luke 24:44-53 and Acts 1:1-11) are already options for Easter 7 in Years A, B and C of the *RCL*, today's readings fittingly invite preachers to connect them to the ascension story.

The selections from John, Psalms and Revelation all speak to the motif of ascension. In John 7, Jesus says, "I will be with you a little while longer, and then I am going to him who sent me. You will search for me, but you will not find me; and where I am, you cannot come" (vv 33-34). Such a reference as this likely refers not only to Jesus' resurrection, but also his ascension into heaven. In Psalm 142, the author, who is being persecuted by enemies and feeling troubled, seeks to be uplifted by God. "Give heed to my cry," the psalmist writes, "for I am brought very low" (v 6). In contrast to this image, Revelation 21 offers a vision of God's kingdom descending from heaven to be with Jesus' disciples in the midst of their persecution. John of Patmos here describes the enormity of the New Jerusalem (a fifteen hundred mile cube) and how the foundations of its walls contain twelve distinctive jewels, representing the fullness of the tribes of Israel. Readings such as these speak to themes of ascension and heaven in ways that transcend the ability of conventional human language to express.

Of all the recommended texts, however, perhaps none better capture the spirit of Ascension Day and the days leading up to it than the reading from Jeremiah 38. In this story, supporters of

King Zedekiah are angry with the prophet Jeremiah over his apparent approval of Israel's Babylonian invaders. With the king's support, they take Jeremiah and lower him into a muddy cistern. As the prophet sinks into the mire, Zedekiah's servant Ebedmelech, an Ethiopian eunuch (perhaps thematically linked to the one later described in Acts 8:26-40) obtains the king's permission to get some helpers to rescue him. They lower rags and clothes down on ropes and tell him how to arrange them so they can lift him out of the pit. Jeremiah's ascension from the cistern represents a "high point" for preachers who have led their parishioners from the inclusive message of Epiphany through the difficult imagery of Lent. Today, they culminate the Easter season with this extraordinary story about a righteous Gentile raising a faithful Jewish prophet from the mud of death to new life. Such a climactic story fittingly celebrates the spirit of Ascension Day, even as Christians look ahead to celebrate the coming of the Holy Spirit next Sunday on Pentecost.

Prayer: Lift us up, God, as we thank you for the promise of heaven and give you glory and praise. May we raise our heads and look to you amid all the difficulties of life. Amen.

Pentecost and Trinity Sundays

Pentecost Sunday
Deuteronomy 16:9-12
Isaiah 60:19-22
Galatians 3:1-5
John 3:31-36

The name "Pentecost," derived from the Greek word meaning "fifty," was originally observed as the Jewish Festival of Weeks, described in Deuteronomy 16 as occurring seven weeks (fifty days) after Passover. Though it was linked to themes of harvest and the giving of the law to Moses at Mt. Sinai, the Christian tradition now views it differently. Despite the testimony of John 20:19-22, in which Jesus' disciples receive the Holy Spirit one week after Easter Sunday, the church traditionally celebrates the Spirit's coming on Pentecost. This is because of the compelling account of the disciples' reception of the Spirit on this day in Acts 2:1-21, which is used for Pentecost Sunday in all three years of the *RCL*. This observance of what is sometimes described as the "birthday" of the church is a testimony to God's wildness, filled with images of wind, sound, and fire. Local churches often celebrate this day with the sacrament of Holy Communion and sometimes the rite of Confirmation.

Today's readings testify to what a powerful gift the Holy Spirit is in people's lives. In Galatians 3, Paul becomes angry with those who insist that men become circumcised before following Jesus. "Are you so foolish?" he asks. "Having started with the Spirit, are you now ending in the flesh?" (v 3). While Paul is contrasting the terms "Spirit" and "flesh" to gain a rhetorical advantage over his "pro-circumcision" opponents, he is also pointing to the reality of Spirit's supremacy over all physical and temporal things. Isaiah 60 also offers a vision of such divine sovereignty, as the prophet writes, "The sun shall no longer be your light by day, nor for brightness shall the moon give light to you by night; but the Lord will be your everlasting light, and your God will be your glory" (v 19). Such glory as this is likely to be the kind of thing Paul wants the Galatians to set their minds on when he asks them, "Does God supply you with the Spirit and work miracles among you by your doing the works of the law, or by your believing what you heard?" (v 5). For Paul, the glory of the Spirit comes from faith in the gospel and not from the observance of ritual or law.

In today's selection from the final verses in John 3, the author offers more testimony about how the Spirit is not an honor to be merited but a powerful gift to be received. This chapter begins with Jesus teaching Nicodemus about the Spirit and ends with the narrator declaring the importance of both Jesus and the Spirit. In v 31, the author writes, "The one who comes from heaven is above all." By saying this, he emphasizes Jesus' sovereignty over the powers of the world. Then, the writer declares, "He whom God has sent speaks the words of God, for he gives the Spirit without measure" (v 34). In this way, the author of John attributes authority not only to Jesus but also to the Spirit whom Jesus endlessly and unsparingly gives. On a day when Christians celebrate how the coming of the Spirit changes people's lives, preachers will do well to explore how God abundantly pours out the gift of the Holy Spirit to build up and empower people in astonishing ways.

Prayer: Thank you, God, for the powerful gift of your Holy Spirit. Amen.

Trinity Sunday
Song of Songs 8:6-7
Psalm 89:5-8
Hebrews 11:4-7, 17-28
John 5:19-24

When the apostle Paul considers spiritual gifts in 1 Corinthians 13, he writes, "And now faith, hope, and love abide, these three; and the greatest of these is love" (v 13). The persons of the Trinity are not the same as "faith, hope and love," but Christian doctrine emphasizes the perfect faith, hope and love that the persons of the Trinity share with one another. Christians, then, are also called to have faith, hope and love in their relationships with God and other people.

Today's scriptures bear this out, particularly in regard to the attributes of faith and love. In terms of faith, the author of Psalm 89 extols God's fidelity by saying, "Let the heavens praise your wonders, O Lord, your faithfulness in the assembly of the holy ones" (v 5). The faithfulness of the ancestors of Israel is also celebrated in the divided reading in Hebrews 11, as the author praises the faith of Abel, Enoch, Noah, Abraham, Isaac, Jacob, Joseph and Moses. The author is making an appeal to these spiritual forbears to show that faith is essential not only for the Jewish people, but also for followers of Jesus. In terms of love, the reading from Song of Songs 8, which is often used at weddings, focuses on human passion. This kind of love offers glimpses of the divine love intimately known by the persons of the Trinity, both for each other and for all creation. John 5 also speaks about the nature of the relationship shared between two of the persons of the Trinity. In traditional Trinitarian language, this passage shows how the Father and Son are united, even though they each have distinct roles. Jesus speaks of their love for each other when he says, "The Father loves the Son and shows him all that he himself is doing" (v 20). In these ways, all of today's readings speak to the importance of the spiritual gifts of faith and love.

As for hope, the whole teaching about the Trinity centers on Christians' hope in a great mystery. The persons of the Trinity are three, yet one. All three persons are divine, but they are not each other. The Bible only hints at the kind of Trinitarian theology that later developed in Christian thought and tradition. Today, people face challenging dilemmas in speaking of the Trinity. For example, the patriarchal character of the persons of the Trinity as they are traditionally understood is problematic, as is the tendency of some to see the members of the Trinity as attributes instead of persons. Some preachers use such images as a cloverleaf (three leaves in one plant), water (three states for one substance) or other models to describe the Trinity, but all human attempts to rationally capture the concept fail. One image that may come closer than others is that of persons in right relationship with each other. It is toward this ideal that Christians look as they discipline themselves in the hope of modeling their relationships with God and one another after the right relationship exemplified by the persons of the Trinity.

Prayer: God in three persons, help us to believe in you even when we cannot fully comprehend you. Inspire us to have the kind of right relationship with you and one another that you reveal to us in your holy Trinity. Amen.

Propers

Proper 1/Epiphany 6

"Propers" refer to parts of the Christian liturgy that vary each year. The calendar annually varies, as do the number of Sundays after Epiphany and Pentecost. In the context of lectionary scriptures, then, propers refer to passages recommended for Sundays that fall within certain calendar dates. There are twenty-nine propers in all, and Proper 1 is to be used on Epiphany 6 if it is not the Sunday before Ash Wednesday (Transfiguration Sunday).

Ezekiel 2:6-3:4

Psalm 3

Revelation 10:1-11

Matthew 13:10-17

Today's readings illustrate ways in which prophets use vivid imagery to teach a message of God's deliverance. Psalm 3, which begins a semi-continuous progression through the book of Psalms, is a prayer for deliverance from enemies. "O Lord," the psalmist prays, "how many are my foes! Many are rising against me" (v 1). This could well have been a cry of the prophet Ezekiel, who was surrounded by enemies. In Ezekiel 2, he hears a voice saying, "Do not be afraid of their words, though briers and thorns surround you and you live among scorpions" (v 6). Ezekiel is clearly stung by his critics' words, and so is Jesus in Matthew 13:10-17. Citing Ezekiel 12:2, Jesus says, "The reason I speak to them in parables is that 'seeing they do not perceive, and hearing they do not listen, nor do they understand'" (v 13). He aims to give his disciples hope in God's deliverance when he says, "To you it has been given to know the secrets of the kingdom of heaven, but to them it has not been given" (v 11).

The readings from Ezekiel 2 and Revelation 10 use scrolls as symbols to describe how God delivers prophets not simply *from* evil but *for* the purpose of proclamation. In the visions described in these passages, divine figures charge Ezekiel and John of Patmos, respectively, to eat scrolls (Ezekiel 3:1-3 and Revelation 10:9-10). For Ezekiel, the scroll tastes "as sweet as honey" (3:3). For John of Patmos "it was sweet as honey in my mouth, but when I had eaten it, my stomach was made bitter" (v 10). After eating the scrolls, both prophets are admonished to speak. A heavenly voice in Ezekiel 3 says, "Mortal, go to the house of Israel and speak my very words to them" (v 4). An angel in Revelation 10 declares, "You must prophesy again about many peoples and nations and languages and kings" (v 11). In both cases, the scroll acts as a parable, or a metaphor, for how they are set free to proclaim what God commands.

Preachers believe that they are called by God to speak, and in order to do this faithfully, they must consume and digest the words of scripture. If they do this well, they come to live and breathe the Bible's message. Dedicated preachers then discover that the act of sermon delivery becomes a "full body/full being" experience. While the words of scripture may taste sweet to them, they may upset their stomachs, as well as those of their hearers. As preachers allow these texts to digest within them, they will want to challenge their parishioners to consume scripture to the point that their very lives, as individuals and as communities of faith, embody the Word.

Prayer: God, set us free from evil so we may consume the scroll you have given us to eat. Help us to digest your message thoroughly so we may faithfully share your good news. Amen.

Proper 2/Epiphany 7

Proper 2 may be used on Epiphany 7 if it is not the Sunday before
Ash Wednesday (Transfiguration Sunday).

1 Samuel 28:7-8, 11-25
Psalm 6
2 Peter 2:1-3, 17-22
Matthew 7:13-17

Today's texts serve as cautionary tales for leaders. Leaders are
entrusted with great responsibilities, and sadly, some misuse
their power and authority. The author of 2 Peter 2 warns against
such abuses, alerting readers to the dangers of false prophets and
teachers by saying, "These are waterless springs and mists
driven by a storm" (v 17). Believing that they are a grave threat
to the unity of the church, the writer pronounces harsh words of
judgment against them. In Matthew 7, Jesus also warns his
hearers in the Sermon on the Mount, "Beware of false prophets
who come to you in sheep's clothing but inwardly are ravenous
wolves. You will know them by their fruits" (vv 15-16). Jesus
wants his followers to be on the watch for those who would
deceive and mislead them.

One of the most interesting warnings against false prophets
and leaders may be found in today's reading in 1 Samuel 28. This
unusual story about Saul's consultation with the medium at
Endor is filled with complexities. Readers may wonder who is
good or evil in this story. Many may find themselves sympa-
thizing with Saul as a man who seems to be grasping at straws as
his world crumbles around him. The medium does not appear to
be vilified in the text. The ghost of Samuel is the one who sounds
merciless, as he condemns Saul for not committing genocide
against the Amalekites. Preachers have an obligation to speak
against such callous, abhorrent violence as this. At the same
time, they should also bring to their hearers' awareness the fact

that Saul's eventual fate reveals that the story's intent is to warn leaders against the dangers of faithlessness.

In many ways, effective leadership can be a healing antidote to spiritual disease. Communities of faith are subject to anxieties that can have crippling effects on their missions. Leaders amplify anxiety among their followers when they do not direct their communities toward their collective mission. Saul and the misguided prophets in 2 Peter 2 and Matthew 17 fail to point their people toward God as their true leader. They lack the vision to see that earthly rulers come and go and are subject to excessive pride, corruption, love of flattery, addiction to power and greed. Today's texts point to the truth that leaders are only effective when they direct others toward fulfilling their shared purpose. In the church, then, leaders must direct others to look beyond themselves to God, their ultimate authority. Many are tempted to turn away from such difficult work, but as Jesus declares in Matthew 7, "The gate is narrow and the way is hard that leads to life" (v 13).

Prayer: As leaders and preachers, teach us how to serve you faithfully. Remind us that our work is about serving you and not about gaining glory for ourselves. Help us to be true to you in the face of every temptation to go astray. Amen.

Proper 3/Epiphany 8

Proper 3 may be used on Epiphany 8 if it is not the Sunday before Ash Wednesday (Transfiguration Sunday) or the Sunday between May 24 and 28 (inclusive) if it is after Trinity Sunday. It is the earliest Sunday in which propers may appear after Trinity Sunday.

Genesis 4:1-16
Psalm 7
Jude 8-13
Matthew 9:32-34

Today's scriptures serve as warnings against arrogance, envy and treachery. In Matthew 9, Jesus drives out a demon from a mute man, but a group of religious leaders, who find their power and privilege threatened by him, vilify him by saying, "By the ruler of the demons he casts out the demons" (v 34). The author of Psalm 7 is also confronted by enemies who "conceive evil, and are pregnant with mischief, and bring forth lies" (v 14). Fearing their violence, the psalmist prays, "Save me from all my pursuers and deliver me, or like a lion they will tear me apart; they will drag me away with no one to rescue" (v 2). The author of Jude similarly confronts a group of teachers who "defile the flesh, reject authority, and slander the glorious ones" (v 8). Jude continues, "They slander whatever they do not understand, and they are destroyed by those things that, like irrational animals, they know by instinct" (v 10). Throughout this letter, the writer offers warnings about the dangers of falling into the traps of these false teachers, comparing their treachery to that of the ancient villain Cain.

The story of Cain and Abel in today's selection from Genesis 4 marks the beginning of a semi-continuous progression of readings through the Hebrew Bible. This difficult text describes the first murder (a fratricide) and its punishment. It begins with

Eve giving birth to Cain, a tiller of the soil, and then Abel, a keeper of sheep. Cain gives God an offering of his produce, and Abel offers part of his flock. For an undisclosed reason, God accepts Abel's offering but rejects Cain's. God warns Cain against the dangers of sin, but the envious Cain lures his brother into a field and kills him. God then confronts Cain, who denies knowing where his brother is. God is not fooled and declares Cain to be "cursed from the ground" (v 11). Cain laments that he has become destined to be a fugitive and wanderer, and he fears that someone will murder him. God places a mark on him so that no one who comes on him will kill him.

This last story raises a compelling and challenging opportunity. Parishioners may wonder how any avenger could threaten Cain if Adam, Eve and their sons were the only people on earth. The answer is that the author is less concerned with consistency than with making certain points. One of these is to explain why, at that time, an agrarian society was overtaking a wandering, nomadic culture. Cain's killing of Abel serves to explain that phenomenon. A deeper, interpersonal point, however, is the ethical warning the story offers against envy and hatred. Preachers have an opportunity to counter these vices by leading with a kind of character that contrasts with the hubris, malice and hatred showed by Cain and others in today's readings.

Prayer: Set us free, God, from envy, hatred and any sin that would consume and destroy us. Deliver us from evil, we pray. Amen.

Proper 4

Proper 4 may be used on the Sunday between May 29 and June 4 (inclusive) if it is after Trinity Sunday.

Genesis 19:1-8, 15-26, 30-38
Psalm 11
2 Peter 2:4-10a
Matthew 11:20-24

The story of Sodom and Gomorrah may be said to inhabit the "collective unconscious" of the Christian faith. It is present in many twenty-first century religious discussions but never occurs on Sundays in the *RCL*. Like other contentious passages selected in this book, the reading offered here is broadened so that interpreters might set it in proper context and clarify the Biblical authors' original intent. The recommended verses from Genesis 19 (a related story is in Judges 19:16-30) begin with Lot encountering two angels, whom he welcomes to his home. When the men of Sodom surround his house, Lot offers them his two virgin daughters in exchange for the angels' safety. The angels urge Lot to leave with his family, and when he lingers, they force him and his family out to the city of Zoar. God rains sulfur and fire on Sodom and Gomorrah, and Lot's wife, upon looking back, turns into a pillar of salt. Lot then moves into a cave with his daughters, who get him drunk, have sex with him, and later give birth to Moab and Ben-ammi.

Today's other readings relate to the Sodom and Gomorrah story. In Matthew 11, Jesus compares certain cities he visits to Tyre, Sidon and Sodom. Of Capernaum, he says, "I tell you that on the day of judgment it will be more tolerable for the land of Sodom than for you" (v 24). The author of 2 Peter 2 compares false teachers in the church to the people of Sodom and Gomorrah. Jude 6-7 makes the same comparison, but 2 Peter 2 does so more extensively. Finally, the writer of Psalm 11 declares, "On the wicked

[God] will rain coals of fire and sulfur" (v 6). Clearly, this is a reference to the Sodom and Gomorrah story in Genesis 19.

While 2 Peter 2 describes Lot as "a righteous man greatly distressed by the licentiousness of the lawless" (v 7), the portrait painted of Lot in Genesis 19 is much more ambiguous. It is true that Lot shows hospitality to the angels in contrast to Sodom's inhospitality. (Sodom's crime here is not homosexuality but attempted rape.) Lot also, however, offers his daughters for rape (v 8), waffles at the counsel of angels (v 16), shows cowardice in the face of danger (v 19) and must have been pretty drunk to be ignorant of committing incest (vv 31-36). These final verses of Genesis 19 are included to show how this story, like others in Genesis, is an explanatory one. In this case, it provides an unfavorable description of the origin of Israel's enemies, the Moabites (descendants of Moab) and Ammonites (descendants of Ben-ammi). It makes the case that Israel's enemies were corrupt from their very beginnings. This may set the rest of the story in context for preachers and hearers who think that the story says one thing when, in fact, it says quite another.

Prayer: God, help us to trust in you in times of distress. Teach us how to look beyond rhetoric so that we may see through to your truth. Amen.

Proper 5
Proper 5 may be used on the Sunday between June 5 and 11 (inclusive) if it is after Trinity Sunday.

Genesis 27:1-10, 18-19, 26-33, 38-40
Psalm 12
Acts 4:23-31
Matthew 17:24-27

Today's texts relate stories of how God provides for people, and how this emboldens them to live out their faith. The author of Psalm 12 asserts God's provision in writing, "The promises of the Lord are promises that are pure, silver refined in a furnace on the ground, purified seven times. You, O Lord, will protect us; you will guard us from this generation forever" (vv 6-7). God's promise and help are further revealed in Matthew 17, where Jesus talks with Peter about a confrontation that he had with some tax collectors about whether or not he paid the temple tax. He tells Peter, "Go to the sea and cast a hook; take the first fish that comes up; and when you open its mouth, you will find a coin; take that and give it to them for you and me" (v 27). Such readings reveal how God provides people ways out of difficult situations.

The remaining texts for this day further amplify the theme of God's provision. In the reading from Acts 4, which begins a semi-continuous progression through the book of Acts, Peter and John overcome a dangerous situation. They are taken before the council of rulers in Jerusalem but are released, and all the disciples respond to the good news by praying. "When they had prayed," v 31 reads, "the place in which they were gathered together was shaken; and they were all filled with the Holy Spirit and spoke the word of God with boldness." In the divided reading from Genesis 27, Jacob exemplifies the quality of boldness. His mother, Rebekah, conspires with him to steal the blessing of her husband, Isaac, from her older son, Esau. While Esau is away, Jacob disguises himself as his brother. Isaac blesses him, and when Esau returns, he laments that his blessing has been taken from him. While this is a tale of provision for Jacob, it is one of deprivation for Esau.

Because of this apparent injustice, Genesis 27 is a problematic text. Its context suggests that readers are to side with Jacob as he tries to get his father's blessing. While he does receive it, people today will likely wonder how his trickery can be ethically justified. The key to understanding this is to read the passage not as a moral tale but an explanatory one. Many stories in Genesis are written to explain things, and in this case, the point is to show why the relationship between the Edomites (Esau's descendants) and the Israelites (Jacob's descendants) is close and tense. It is a polemical piece against the Edomites, and it is unusual in that it shows Jacob (Israel) deposing his brother not by reason of his strength but by his wits. The author of this text is not claiming that Israel is mighty and powerful but that it is clever. If those who hear this passage are clever enough to see how God's providing hand is at work in their lives, maybe they, too, will be emboldened to live as people who know how blessed they are.

> Prayer: God, open our minds to discern how you provide for our needs. Help us to trust in you so that we may be emboldened to live as people who are blessed by your hand. Amen.

Proper 6

Proper 6 may be used on the Sunday between June 12 and 18 (inclusive) if it is after Trinity Sunday.

Genesis 38:1-26

Psalm 35:19-25

Acts 5:1-11

Matthew 12:43-45

Today's readings show that evil multiplies in the world, and the New Testament texts illustrate this reality well. In Matthew 12, Jesus describes what happens to an unclean spirit when it leaves someone. He compares such a person to a house and describes how an evil spirit eventually returns, bringing more spirits with it. "The last state of that person is worse than the first" (v 45), he says. The last state of the married couple Ananias and Sapphira in Acts 5 is likely to be worse than they could have imagined.

They sell a piece of land and conspire to keep part of the money while claiming to give it all to the disciples. Peter catches Ananias in the lie, and Ananias drops over dead. Later, Sapphira arrives and persists in the lie. When Peter confronts her, she dies, too. Readers of this story today can better grasp (but not excuse) the violence in it by understanding that the author (Luke) is using it as way of establishing the disciples' authority.

Another challenging passage in which evil multiplies is the bizarre reading from Genesis 38. It begins with the story of Onan, who fails to inseminate his late brother's wife, Tamar. By spilling his semen on the ground, Onan refuses to do what would have been considered his brotherly duty, and God strikes him dead as a result. Though some commentators wrongly see this text as a prohibition against masturbation, the real issue at hand is Onan's failure to do his duty for his family. This story is followed by that of Tamar's relationship with her father-in-law, Judah. He also fails to do his familial duty because he does not marry her to his youngest son, Shelah. Tamar disguises herself as a prostitute and seduces Judah, taking his signet, cord and staff as collateral. When she is found to be pregnant, he calls for her execution. After Tamar produces his possessions, however, he relents. What bothers him, however, is not his role in prostitution or his double standard in calling for her execution but the fact that he didn't marry her to Shelah. Injustice seems to follow injustice in this story that seems to have little to say of edifying, redeeming or spiritual value.

Psalm 35 is a prayer that those who cry out against the psalmist may not be victorious. "Do not let them say to themselves," the author writes, "'Aha, we have our heart's desire.' Do not let them say, 'We have swallowed him up'" (v 25). In these times, when mainline and/or progressive Christians are assailed by fundamentalists on the one side and atheists on the other, today's texts may cause people to question and even give up faith in a God who either condones or perpetrates the kinds of acts these readings describe. Nonetheless, the Bible is a human work, and human beings have, from the beginning, inhabited a world in which the multiplication of evils is a tragic reality. Preachers have an opportunity with these texts to urge parishioners to resist the evil that seeks to multiply within them.

Prayer: God, teach us to have faith in you and resist the powers of evil. Amen.

Proper 7

Proper 7 may be used on the Sunday between June 19 and 25 (inclusive) if it is after Trinity Sunday.

Genesis 41:9-40
Psalm 37:23-28a
Acts 6:1-7
Mark 8:14-21

Themes of bread and food are inescapable in today's recommended readings. The longest of these texts, found in Genesis 41, requires preachers to provide some background for parishioners to fully understand what is happening. In Genesis 39, Joseph is imprisoned because of Potiphar's wife's wrongful accusations of sexual assault. In Genesis 40, Joseph accurately interprets the dreams of Pharaoh's chief baker and cupbearer. The latter is restored to his position and hears that Pharaoh has been having troubling dreams. Today's reading in chapter 41 begins with the chief cupbearer remembering Joseph's gift of dream interpretation and sharing this information with Pharaoh. Pharaoh summons Joseph out of prison and describes his unusual dreams of cows and corn. Joseph interprets them as meaning that Egypt will undergo seven years of famine, and he advises Pharaoh to store food so the people will have enough when the famine arrives. Because this advice was so critical to the survival of

Egypt, Pharaoh rewards Joseph by appointing him second-in-command.

The remaining scriptures also contain abundant food imagery. Acts 6 describes how the disciples choose seven men to serve as deacons who wait on tables in a spirit of hospitality. The theme of feeding is also advanced in Psalm 37, in which the author says, "I have been young, and now and old, yet I have not seen the righteous forsaken or their children begging bread" (v 25). Finally, in the Gospel text, now from Mark 8, Jesus warns the disciples, who have forgotten to bring bread with them, to "beware of the yeast of the Pharisees and the yeast of Herod" (v 15). When they think he is talking about their lack of bread, he calls to mind their experience earlier in chapter 8 of the feeding of the four thousand (selected on Easter 5). "Do you not yet understand?" (v 21) he asks them.

The consistent imagery of bread and food in these readings makes this a good Sunday for preachers to focus on food issues. For churches that do not commune each Sunday, these texts serve as prophetic reminders of Christians' continuous need to be nourished by the bread that Christ offers. If there are hunger ministries that the church supports, today would be an opportune time to emphasize them. Such ethical issues as fair wages for global producers, just treatment of animals and concerns about marketing unhealthy and chemically altered food may be options for preachers to examine. Today's world is one in which food issues abound, from eating disorders to malnutrition. As the church strives to respond faithfully to injustice in the world, preachers will do well to point out how these texts show that God gives people physical and spiritual bread that is truly nourishing and life-sustaining.

Prayer: Thank you, God, for feeding us with your life-giving bread. Having been nourished by you, help us to reach out to others in a spirit of love and service. Amen.

Proper 8

Proper 8 may be used on the Sunday between June 26 and July 2 (inclusive).

Exodus 32:15-34

Psalm 44:1-3

Acts 7:35-43

Mark 7:9-13

The consequences of idol worship are dramatically portrayed in Exodus 32 (a related story is in 1 Kings 12:25-33), a complex chapter that is likely to be the product of several authors and editors. It begins with a description of the story of the Golden Calf in vv 1-14, which is used on Proper 23 in Year A (and in part on Proper 19 of Year C) of the *RCL*. Today's text, which is the first in a series of three Hebrew Bible readings that emphasize the authority of Moses, reveals what happens after the Israelites become idolatrous in vv 1-14. First, Moses destroys the tablets of the covenant when he hears the sound of the people's revelry. After this, he listens to Aaron's comic defense of the idol's creation: "I said to them, 'Whoever has gold, take it off; so they gave it to me, and I threw it into the fire, and out came this calf!'" (v 24). Moses then commands the Levites, "Go back and forth from gate to gate throughout the camp, and each of you kill your brother, your friend, and your neighbor" (v 27). While preachers will recoil at the thought of such slaughter, they may also explain that there were times in Jewish history when the priesthoods of Aaron and Levi came into conflict. The authors' representation of Aaron as weak and ineffectual reveals their disdain for the Aaronic priests, and their depiction of the Levites as righteous avengers shows their support of Levi's tribe. While preachers may address this, they will not want to lose sight of the authors' broader warnings against practicing idolatry.

Such warnings are also emphasized in today's other readings.

In Acts 7, Stephen relates a history of Israel to the Council in Jerusalem, focusing particularly on the activity of Moses. He first describes Moses' role in the Exodus event and then, in vv 39-40, speaks disparagingly of the people's idolatry. In Mark 7, Jesus addresses ways in which people turn from God in his day. "You have a fine way," he exclaims, "of rejecting the commandment of God in order to keep your tradition!" (v 9). He attacks their belief that calling something "Corban," or offered to God, is a valid excuse for failing to keep God's commandments. Finally, Psalm 44 reflects on the goodness that God showed to the ancestors of Israel. Such goodness serves as a contrast to the disobedience depicted among the people in today's other readings.

Preachers of these texts might choose to speak against modern idolatries, but they may also focus on the broader dangers of falling into the same traps as their ancestors. Churches are communities of memory, and stories from their past shape and give meaning to their present struggles. Connecting the biblical past with the histories of local churches may bring to people's awareness insights that preach effectively and promote healing and growth. Such preaching will remind churches that they are not prisoners of the past but are free to faithfully turn to God today.

Prayer: God, we pray that we might learn wisely from the errors that our ancestors made. Remind us that you set us free from the past to be faithful to you in the present. Amen.

Proper 9

Proper 9 may be used on the Sunday between July 3 and 9 (inclusive).

Numbers 12:1-15
Psalm 53
Acts 12:6-19
Luke 14:2-6

Today's texts move from despair to healing and hope. The author of Psalm 53 declares that all have turned from God. "They have all fallen away," the psalmist laments, "they are all alike perverse; there is no one who does good, no, not one" (v 3). The psalm ends, however, with a word of hope in v 7, which reads, "When God restores the fortunes of his people, Jacob will rejoice; Israel will be glad." Today's selection from Numbers 12 similarly moves from anguish to healing. In this text, Aaron and Moses' sister, Miriam, insist that God speaks to them, not just to Moses. God angrily responds to this by turning Miriam leprous. Aaron then asks Moses to plead to God on her behalf, which he does. God responds by commanding that she be shut out of the camp for a week. "If her father had but spit in her face," God says, "would she not bear her shame for seven days?" (v 14). Preachers may wrestle with how cruel and sexist God sounds here, and they may help their listeners to understand (though not excuse) this by explaining that the Biblical author is using this story to emphasize the importance of Moses' authority. The story concludes on a note of hope, as a healed Miriam is reintegrated into the camp and the people move on toward the Promised Land.

The New Testament readings today also deal with issues of healing, deliverance and restoration. As the Gospel texts move into Luke, the verses in chapter 14 relate how Jesus heals a man of the swelling disease of dropsy. Some question him because he does this on a sabbath, but Jesus urges them to be compassionate. "If one of you has a child or an ox that has fallen into a well" he says, "will you not immediately pull it out on a sabbath day?" (v 5). In saying this, he seeks to liberate people's view of sabbath by showing it to be a joyful opportunity instead of a burdensome obligation. The story of Rhoda in Acts 12 also relates a message of liberation. An angel frees Peter from prison, and he goes to the home of a disciple named Mary. Rhoda, the maid, is so excited to see him at the door that she forgets to open it. Instead, she rushes to tell the other disciples about his arrival, but they doubt her and think she is mad. Meanwhile, Peter keeps knocking, and they eventually let him in and hear about how God set him free.

While it may be tempting to laugh at Rhoda's antics and dismiss her as a "Biblical airhead," her story reveals something critical about faith. It is one thing to passively reflect on how God delivers people but quite another to catch the sense of excitement and joy that Rhoda must have felt when she saw that Peter was free. Christians may seek to be reverent in worship, but how often have they been so thrilled by God's liberating work that they, like Rhoda, forget where they are? By sharing this relatively unknown story from the Bible, preachers can show an enthusiasm for experiencing God that hopefully will be contagious in their churches.

Prayer: God, thank you for healing us and setting us free. Amaze and astound us, so that we lose ourselves in your praise. Amen.

Proper 10

Proper 10 may be used on the Sunday between July 10 and 16 (inclusive).

Numbers 16:1-5, 23-35

Psalm 55

Acts 14:8-18

John 2:23-25

Today's readings serve as warnings against unfaithfulness and disobedience. In Numbers 16, Korah, Dathan and Abiram accuse Moses of making an exclusive claim to God's holiness. Moses is so filled with anguish when he hears of their rebellion that he falls on his face. He meets with them, and as he speaks, the earth opens up and swallows them, along with their families. As has been the case with the Hebrew Bible readings over the past several weeks, preachers shocked by the violence (and apparent anti-egalitarianism) in this story may note the interest its composers had in validating Moses' authority. Similarly, the author of Psalm 55 tries to claim divine authority against betrayers. The psalmist may have had Numbers 16 in mind in lamenting, "It is not my enemies who taunt me - I could bear that; it is not adversaries who deal insolently with me - I could hide from them. But it is you, my equal, my companion, my familiar friend, with whom I kept pleasant company; we walked in the house of God with the throng. Let death come upon them; let them go down alive to Sheol; for evil is in their homes and in their hearts" (vv 12-15). Betrayal in the faith community is even more painful than it is in the secular world because of the expectation that things should be different there.

The New Testament readings for this Sunday also warn against the human proclivity to turn away from God. Today begins a long, semi-continuous progression in the Gospel of John with a few brief verses from chapter 2. Jesus is in Jerusalem for the Passover festival, having just driven the money changers out of the temple. The author of John reveals Jesus' insight into human nature by testifying, "But Jesus on his part would not entrust himself to them, because he knew all people and needed no one to testify about anyone; for he himself knew what was in everyone" (vv 24-25). Another story depicting the frailty of human character is today's reading about Paul and Barnabas in Acts 14. While in Lystra, they see a man who never walked, and Paul commands him to stand. The man rises and walks, and when the crowds see it, they call Paul "Hermes" and Barnabas "Zeus." The two disciples try to keep the people from making them into idols as they testify to God's working through them. "Even with these words," Luke writes, "they scarcely restrained the crowds from offering sacrifice to them" (v. 18).

Today's readings warn against human inclinations toward idolatry and rebellion, but they also point to an important truth for pastoral leaders. When Moses struggles with leading the people, he turns to God for help. When Paul and Barnabas face the deifying accolades of the crowd, they deflect the praise toward God. Even the psalmist turns to God when facing the acute pains of betrayal. The theme of leading by pointing away from self and toward God is a healing message for pastors and congregations to hear, especially in times of crisis or despair.

Prayer: God, when our will to wander away from you is strong, help us to turn and look to you for leadership in the challenges of our lives. Amen.

Proper 11

Proper 11 may be used on the Sunday between July 17 and 23 (inclusive).

Judges 6:11-18, 36-40
Psalm 61
Acts 19:11-16
John 5:10-18

Today's readings deal with a variety of challenges to God's authority, and the New Testament texts specifically address questions about the authority of Jesus. In John 5, Jesus is interrogated by religious leaders who persecute him for healing on the sabbath. Verse 18 states that they "were seeking all the more to kill him, because he was not only breaking the sabbath, but was also calling God his own Father, therefore making himself equal to God." Further challenges to Jesus' authority emerge in Acts 19, when some itinerant Jewish exorcists, seven sons of a high priest, Sceva, attempt to cast out evil spirits "by the Jesus whom Paul proclaims" (v 13). The spirit replies to them, "Jesus I know, and Paul I know; but who are you?" (v 15). The man with the evil spirit overpowers them, and they flee. This passage reinforces the authority of Jesus and his followers while confounding those who are not true disciples and merely want to use his name as a magical incantation to get their way. Both New Testament readings show how Jesus is vindicated over those who do not follow him.

In today's divided reading from Judges 6, Gideon also questions God's authority. Gideon is called by an angel to lead the Israelites over the Midianites, but as soon as he is called, he protests. "But sir," he asks, "how can I deliver Israel? My clan is the weakest in Manasseh, and I am the least in my family" (v15). Even though the angel assures him, Gideon equivocates, "If now I have found favor with you, then show me a sign that it is you who speak with me" (v 17). He then makes a deal with the angel, declaring, "I am going to lay a fleece of wool on the threshing floor; if there is dew on the fleece alone, and it is dry on all the ground, then I shall know that you will deliver Israel by my hand, as you have said" (v 37). Even though this happens, Gideon is still skeptical and decides to test God another night, saying, "Let it be dry only on the fleece and on all the ground let there be dew" (v 39). When this occurs, Gideon apparently decides to quit questioning and start believing.

The temptation to test God is a great challenge for people of faith. So many terrible things happen in this world that it is hard to believe that God is real, let alone that God is, as the author of Psalm 61 proclaims, "a strong tower against the enemy" (v 3). It is tempting for people to cut deals in which they agree to do good if God brings good things to them, but then if evil comes their way, they think God must be a big phony. It is they, however, who have set God up in a fraudulent bargain, and the truth is that faith often makes life harder instead of easier. When Jesus is tempted by the devil, he quotes Deuteronomy 6:16 and says to Satan, "Do not put the Lord your God to the test" (Matthew 4:7 and Luke 4:12). If people have tested God in this way, however, Gideon's story may provide them some consolation. If God is patient with Gideon, God will be patient with them, as well.

Prayer: God, help us to respond to you faithfully as our ultimate authority. Amen.

Proper 12

Proper 12 may be used on the Sunday between July 24 and 30 (inclusive).

Judges 7:2-8, 19-23
Psalm 83
Acts 19:21-41
John 5:25-29

Today's readings proclaim the power of God's deliverance, and the New Testament texts demonstrate this explicitly. In Acts 19, a silversmith named Demetrius rouses the people of Ephesus against Paul and the disciples. Demetrius makes shrines to the goddess Artemis, and he is afraid that the followers of Jesus will put him out of business if they succeed in their mission. He rallies the crowd to the cry, "Great is Artemis of the Ephesians!" (v 28) and they continue this chant for hours. Before they do any violence to the disciples, however, they are dismissed by the town clerk, who warns, "We are in danger of being charged with rioting today, since there is no cause that we can give to justify this commotion" (v 40). In John 5, Jesus speaks of the ultimate deliverance of God's people by declaring, "Very truly, I tell you, the hour is coming, and is now here, when the dead will hear the voice of the Son of God, and those who hear will live" (v 25). These passages offer Christians everywhere the comforting assurance that God delivers them from harm and even death.

Today's Hebrew Bible readings also speak to the theme of God's deliverance. Psalm 83 is a prayer for deliverance from the enemies of Israel, as the psalmist exhorts God, "Do to them as you did to Midian," (v 9). Today's reading from Judges 7 relates the story of how God rescued Israel from Midian. In verses 2-8, God commands Gideon to send home everyone who is afraid, and the troops are narrowed from 22,000 to 10,000. Then God brings them down to the water and commands that those who kneel and use their hands to drink should be sent home. Gideon keeps the 300 men who lap water like dogs. In vv 19-23, God sends these troops to the outskirts of the Midianite camp, and at Gideon's command they blow trumpets, break jars and rout the Midianites.

Although the story of the destruction of the Midianites and the prayer of Psalm 83 are problematic examples of religious violence (a theme which preachers might address here), they speak also of God's vindication. In the case of Judges 7, the story of how God gives the Israelites victory is compelling. God says to Gideon, "The troops with you are too many for me to give the Midianites into their hand. Israel would only take the credit away from me, saying, 'My own hand has delivered me'" (v 2). In times when many parishioners are overwhelmed and do not feel like following God, preachers can point to these texts as sources of inspiration that show how God saves and delivers people everywhere from seemingly impossible situations.

Prayer: God, remind us, when it seems as though the world is against us, that you give us victory not by our hands but by yours. Help us to trust in your promise of deliverance. Amen.

Proper 13
Proper 13 may be used on the Sunday between July 31 and August 6 (inclusive).

Judges 16:1-5, 16-31
Psalm 119:17-24
Acts 20:7-12
John 6:37-40

The readings for this day weave together themes of betrayal, falling, deliverance and new life, and the Hebrew Bible selections exemplify these motifs. Psalm 119, the longest chapter in the Bible, is an acrostic, meaning that different verses correspond to the letters of the (Hebrew) alphabet. Today's selection starts a progression through the verses in Psalm 119 that are omitted by the *RCL*. It tells of the psalmist's devotion to God's law, even in the face of betrayal. "Even though princes sit plotting against me," the author writes, "your servant will meditate on your statutes" (v 23). The other Hebrew Bible text from Judges 16 (a variant exists in chapter 14) relates a classic tale of betrayal, the story of Samson and Delilah. This divided reading begins with the story of how Samson falls in love with Delilah, who conspires with the Philistines to betray him. Delilah coaxes Samson's secret from him and tells the Philistines that his strength lies in his hair. They shave his head, blind him, tie him with cords, bring him into the temple of their god, Dagon, and force him to entertain them. Samson prays, grabs the temple's pillars, and with one last burst of strength destroys the building, killing himself and many Philistines. Both of these texts convey the hurt of betrayal as well as the power of God's deliverance.

The New Testament readings also speak about falls (or descents) as well as resurrection. Acts 20 relates the story of Eutychus, a young man who sits in a window and listens to Paul preach into the night. "Overcome by sleep," vv 9-10 read, "he fell to the ground three floors below and was picked up dead. But Paul went down, and bending over him took him in his arms, and said, 'Do not be alarmed, for his life is in him.'" Paul leaves and the text concludes, "Meanwhile they had taken the boy away alive and were not a little comforted" (v 12). In John 6, Jesus also offers his disciples a comforting message related to descents and ascents. He says, "For I have come down from heaven, not to do my own will, but the will of him who sent me. And this is the will of him who sent me, that I should lose nothing of all that he has given me, but raise it up on the last day" (vv 38-39). In these ways, today's readings speak to the new life God gives people.

Life is filled with betrayals, falls and tragedies, and the stories of Delilah's treachery and Eutychus' fall dramatically portray this disastrous side of life. Parishioners will relate to such catastrophes but will also be relieved to hear that today's stories do not end in despair. Samson's final feat of strength proves to be an act of deliverance for Israel, and Eutychus' recovery from death points to the life-giving message Paul proclaims. In John 6:40, Jesus says, "This is indeed the will of my Father, that all who see the Son and believe in him may have eternal life; and I will raise them up on the last day." This testimony of Jesus gives Christians hope that God will deliver them from life's tragedies and ultimately lead them into new life.

Prayer: God, we praise you for coming to us when we fall and raising us to life. Amen.

Proper 14

Proper 14 may be used on the Sunday between August 7 and 13 (inclusive).

2 Samuel 13:1-20, 27b-29
Psalm 119:25-32
1 Corinthians 5:1-5
John 7:1-9

Family life is filled with complex and difficult situations, and the texts for this day show some of the ugliest and most painful ones in the Bible. The author of Psalm 119 sets the stage for today's readings by saying, "My soul clings to the dust; revive me according to your word" (v 25). These passages offer harrowing descriptions of family life that will leave people yearning for revival and hope. In John 7, for example, Jesus' brothers, who do not believe in him, urge him to go to the Festival of Booths. After refusing, he tells them, "The world cannot hate you, but it hates me because I testify against it that its works are evil" (v 8). It is ironic that the one Christians look to for healing and acceptance was hated by the world and rejected by his family.

The remaining texts describe dysfunctional families facing scandals of lust, sex, rape, incest, and in one case, fratricide. 2 Samuel 13 relates a horrific tale about David's son Amnon's plot to have sex with his half-sister Tamar. When his plan fails, he rapes her and casts her out. Tamar's full brother Absalom hears about it and receives her into his house. He then throws a feast to which he invites Amnon, who gets drunk. Absalom orders his half-brother's murder, and his servants carry out his wishes. The day's Epistle reading from 1 Corinthians 5 (the first in a series of selections from Paul's letters) is also a story of incest. Paul chastises the Corinthians, "It is actually reported that there is sexual immorality among you, and of a kind that is not found even among pagans; for a man is living with his father's wife. And you are arrogant!" (vv 1-2). Paul is apparently describing a sexual relationship between the man and his stepmother, and he is angry with the church about it. "When you are assembled," he says, "and my spirit is present with the power of our Lord Jesus, you are to hand this man over to Satan for the destruction of the flesh, so that his spirit may be saved in the day of the Lord" (vv 4-5). Despite Paul's wording here, his verdict is not death but excommunication (as noted in vv 11-13). These texts exhibit the range of challenges severely dysfunctional families and communities face.

An essential part of pastoral ministry is working with families in crisis. When families become aware that intervention is needed, they are often open to seeking pastoral care. Even generally healthy families experience periods of dysfunction when they need outside assistance, and at such times, the church can help them move beyond shrouds of secrecy. Such interventions may determine whether a crisis escalates into tragedy or relaxes and resolves. 1 Samuel 13 is an example of the former, while 1 Corinthians 5 is, in the end, an instance of the latter.

While excommunication is by no means viewed today as effective family therapy, Paul's use of it then helped to lead that church through its crisis and ultimately empowered the man to be restored to the community (as shown in 2 Corinthians 2 in Proper 20). In these ways, today's texts offer hope for those who minister to families in distress.

Prayer: God, when we face crises in our families and churches, heal us. Amen.

Proper 15

Proper 15 may be used on the Sunday between August 14 and 20 (inclusive).

2 Samuel 16:20-17:7, 11-14, 23
Psalm 119:41-48
1 Corinthians 11:2-16
John 7:10-18

Today's selections, including those from the Hebrew Bible, emphasize not only the importance of honor but also the negative consequences of shame. In the selection from Psalm 119, for example, the author writes, "I will also speak of your decrees before kings and will not be put to shame" (v 46). By speaking about the honorable authority of God's law, the psalmist avoids being branded with shame. The other Hebrew Bible reading depicts the vicious downside of shame. 2 Samuel 16 and 17 relate the saga of the counselor Ahithophel, who betrays King David in order to serve David's rebellious son Absalom. Ahithophel, who is widely honored for his wise counsel, advises Absalom to shame his father by publicly having sex with David's concubines. When Absalom needs some crucial military advice, however, he listens to Hushai, a spy of David's, instead of Ahithophel. Ahithophel is so shamed by Absalom's rejection that he sets his house in order and hangs himself. This suicide emphasizes the tragic power shame can have over people's lives.

Today's Epistle reading addresses the subjects of honor and shame in a convoluted way. In 1 Corinthians 11, Paul insists that women should have long hair and wear head coverings in worship and that men should have short hair and worship with their heads uncovered. His argument contains appeals to women's subordination (v 3), cultural notions of honor (vv 4-7), an interpretation of Genesis 3 (vv 8-9 and 11-12), an odd reference to angels (v 10), nature (vv 12-15), and a general assertion that this is how it is (v 16). Paul seems to grasp at straws in an unconvincing argument, and readers may wonder why he does this. An explanation may be found in the fact that when Paul wrote his early letters (such as Galatians), he emphasized the freedom Christians had in Jesus. The Corinthian church, however, took that freedom to extremes, and because of this Paul is anxious in 1 Corinthians 11 to restore a sense of order to it. This is why his argument about honor and shame is so scattered.

Thankfully, today's Gospel reading gives preachers some clear direction in terms of thinking about what is truly honorable in Christian life. In John 7, Jesus decides to secretly attend the Festival of Booths, but midway through it he goes into the temple and teaches. His opponents try to shame him by saying he has a demon, but he asserts a position of honor by claiming to seek God's glory instead of his own. He says, "Those who speak on their own seek their own glory; but the one who seeks the glory of him who sent him is true, and there is nothing false in him" (v 18). For Jesus, God's glory triumphs over every human accolade. In times like these when love of honor and fear of shame still strongly motivate people, preachers will honor these texts when they show that God's glory is to be sought over all human praise.

Prayer: God, teach us to seek your glory over all the honor of this world. Amen.

Proper 16

Proper 16 may be used on the Sunday between August 21 and 27 (inclusive).

1 Kings 3:16-28
Psalm 119:49-56
1 Corinthians 14:6-19
John 7:19-24

Some think of wisdom as a type of knowledge that only few possess, but today's readings show that wise judgment is by no means a secret but is available to all and should be sought by all. The author of Psalm 119, for instance, shows an open love of the wisdom that God reveals in the law. "Your statutes have been my songs wherever I make my home," (v 54) the psalmist writes. Also, in John 7, Jesus confronts the religious authorities who claim that he has a demon. "Do not judge by appearances," he says, "but judge with right judgment" (v 24). Additionally, 1 Kings 3 relates a powerful tale about the availability of wisdom and the importance of just judgment. Earlier in the chapter, a young King Solomon asks God for wisdom, and God grants his prayer. Today's selection tells how Solomon wisely adjudicates a case involving two prostitutes who have newborn sons. One of the women claims that the other laid on her son, killed him and then exchanged babies with her while she slept. The other claims that the living son is hers. The king calls for a sword and commands that the living child be cut in half, with each half given to each woman. One woman objects, while the other agrees. Solomon halts the child's execution and gives him to the woman who protests the verdict. Such readings as these reveal that wisdom is not something that is concealed but is available to those who seek it and precious to those who find it.

Today's reading from 1 Corinthians 14 also demonstrates the truth that wise discernment is not an elusive secret. Paul has been debating people in Corinth who see themselves as free, strong and wise "super-apostles." They claim to have special, secret wisdom which makes them superior to others. Paul consistently takes the side of their "weak" and "foolish" opponents, not because he begrudges the super-apostles' freedom but because he senses that they lack love for their "weak" brothers and sisters. This is why he addresses the subject of speaking in tongues (other languages, real or invented), a practice foreign to many in mainline churches today. Although he approves of this gift in general, he disapproves of those who use it to divide instead of to unite. "In church," he says, "I would rather speak five words with my mind, in order to instruct others, than ten thousand words in a tongue" (v 18). Paul believes that all spiritual gifts should be used to build people up, not create elitist walls of separation between them.

This story highlights the trouble with theologies of secret wisdom. Such beliefs in churches create an elitist (gnostic) class in which those who have special knowledge or experience claim to be saved in a way that others are not. While Paul does not condemn speaking in tongues, he does warn of the dangers of elitism and the divisions that accompany it. Preachers today can cite these texts as examples of how God makes wisdom desirable and accessible, not only to a small group of secret-keepers, but to all people.

Prayer: Thank you, God, for teaching us wisdom, a gift you make available to all. Amen.

Proper 17

Proper 17 may be used on the Sunday between August 28 and September 3 (inclusive).

1 Kings 12:1-20
Psalm 119:57-64
Romans 7:7-13
John 7:40-44

One of the biggest challenges facing the church and the world today is the problem of division, and today's readings vividly illustrate the perils of divisiveness. The Epistle readings shift now to Romans, a letter in which Paul writes about spiritual forces that cause internal strife. In chapter 7, he addresses his inner conflict between wanting to do good while actually doing evil. For Paul, this personal struggle reflects a greater conflict that he sees within the law. He views it as a source of good, but because of its prohibitive character, he also sees within it the seeds of evil. On the one hand, he praises the law when he says, "So the law is holy, and the commandment is holy and just and good" (v 11). In this way, he agrees with the author of Psalm 119, whose praise of the law continues in today's selection. On the other hand, Paul also describes how sin works through the law to do evil when he writes, "For sin, seizing an opportunity in the commandment, deceived me and through it killed me" (v 11). Such insights as these reveal how spiritual forces create divisions within people.

The remaining readings show how division also occurs between people. In John 7, the people are divided about Jesus, with some claiming that he is the Messiah and others wanting to arrest him. The reading from the 1 Kings 12 describes how Israel divided into two nations. Solomon's son, King Rehoboam, hears the pleas of his people to lighten their burdens. His older counselors tell him to listen to the people while his younger friends advise him to respond arrogantly. Rehoboam foolishly listens to his friends and tells his people, "My father disciplined you with whips, but I will discipline you with scorpions" (v 11). The people turn against him, and every tribe except Judah makes Jeroboam their king. In this way, Israel is divided into the Northern Kingdom of Israel and the Southern Kingdom of Judah. Those who read this story can clearly see the destructiveness of this kind of division.

In church and society, there are times when civil discourse breaks down under the weight of dividing forces. In Protestantism today, people disaffected by developments in their traditions are splitting off in ways that continue to harm and fragment the church. Some are forming alliances that threaten to turn Protestantism into competing groups of social conservatives and social liberals, each claiming their view of Jesus to be uniquely authoritative. Such an outcome would be a calamity, because the Christian church is not and never has been a group of like-minded people. Instead, it is a group of unlike-minded people who live out their faith and practice discipleship together. Its aim is not to make everyone happy but to engage people in Jesus' mission. Preachers will do well to proclaim that the source of Christian unity is Jesus, whose position on the cross reveals arms stretched out to those on his right and those on his left.

Prayer: God, help us to work together for Christian unity. Amen.

Proper 18

Proper 18 may be used on the Sunday between September 4 and 10 (inclusive).

Jeremiah 28:1-4, 10-17

Psalm 119:65-72

Romans 14:13-23

John 7:45-52

Today's readings, beginning with those in the Hebrew Bible, emphasize the importance of humility in exercising leadership. The author of Psalm 119 writes, "It is good for me that I was humbled, so that I might learn your statutes" (v 71). Indeed, today's progression in the Hebrew Bible (where, unlike the Christian Old Testament, prophetic writings precede wisdom literature) continues with a reading from Jeremiah 28 that highlights the importance of humility. In this selection, the prophet Hananiah predicts the fall of the Babylonian kingdom that has now conquered Israel. He takes the symbolic yoke of Israel's oppression that Jeremiah carries and breaks it. God later tells Jeremiah that Hananiah has spoken falsely. Hananiah's arrogance in claiming to speak for God presumably rises out a desire to ingratiate himself to the people with a popular message. "Listen, Hananiah," Jeremiah says, "the Lord has not sent you, and you made this people trust in a lie" (v 15). Jeremiah predicts Hananiah's death, and when it occurs later that year, his hearers are undoubtedly reminded of the dangers of arrogance.

The New Testament readings today also serve as exhortations to humility. In Romans 14, Paul declares, "Let us therefore no longer pass judgment on one another, but resolve instead never to put a stumbling block or hindrance in the way of another" (v 13). In the Roman church, a group of elites are feeling free to eat and drink in ways that wound the consciences of others in their church. As he does in 1 Corinthians 8 (see Epiphany 4 in Year B of the *RCL*), Paul takes the side of those who are hurt by the elites' freedom. He is interested in building up the church as a whole and tells the Romans, "Let us then pursue what makes for peace and for mutual upbuilding" (v 19). In John 7, the religious leaders of Jesus' day accuse the crowds who sympathize with Jesus of not knowing the law. Nicodemus, who visited Jesus by night in John 3, retorts that the law allows for hearings. The leaders, however, silence him by saying, "Search and you will see that no prophet is to arise from Galilee" (v 52). The irony of this statement is not lost on Christians, from John's time to today, who know who Jesus really is for them.

This final reading is perhaps the biggest cautionary word to preachers who are tempted to have all the answers. Because people project onto pastors the unrealistic expectation that they should know the answers to life's mysteries, those who are reluctant to show their ignorance claim to speak for God in ways that are untrue. Fueled by the need to ingratiate themselves with some, they may even misuse their leadership role to "put others in their place" in a way that is contrary to the spirit of today's readings. As the religious leaders of Jesus' day tried to silence him because they thought they knew better, pastors today should beware that, in their quest to justify themselves in their positions, they do not do the same.

Prayer: God, grant us humility in leadership so we may proclaim your truth. Amen.

Proper 19

Proper 19 may be used on the Sunday between September 11 and 17 (inclusive).

Jeremiah 32:36-44
Psalm 119:73-80
2 Corinthians 1:3-11
John 7:53-8:11

While *Beyond the Lectionary* prescribes some difficult scriptures, it also recommends such passages of hope and inspiration as those that are offered today. In Psalm 119, the writer declares, "Those who fear you shall see me and rejoice, because I have hoped in your word" (v 74). Also, one of the most hopeful writings in all the prophets is found in today's selection from Jeremiah 32. As Israel braces for exile into Babylonia, God promises, "I will make an everlasting covenant with them, never to draw back from doing good to them; and I will put the fear of me in their hearts, so that they may not turn from me. I will rejoice in doing good to them, and I will plant them in this land in faithfulness, with all my heart and soul" (vv 40-41). God promises that fields will be bought and sold in the land again, and this gives hope to a people on the brink of despair.

The suggested New Testament readings also overflow with a message of hope. In the Epistle text, a semi-continuous progression begins in 2 Corinthians, one of Paul's most defensive yet fascinating writings. In today's selection from chapter 1, which is often used in funeral liturgies, Paul blesses and consoles the Corinthians because they have been deeply concerned about the sufferings he and other disciples faced on a recent journey to Asia. Paul lifts their spirits by saying, "He who rescued us from so deadly a peril will continue to rescue us; on him we have set our hope that he will rescue us again" (v 10). Such a message of hopeful deliverance also resounds in today's Gospel reading in

John 8. This selection was probably not included in the *RCL* because, as many Bibles accurately footnote, scholars doubt its originality. Nonetheless, this story about a woman caught in adultery is one of the most profound texts in all of scripture and captures the heart of the Gospel message that Jesus proclaims. Religious leaders bring this woman to Jesus and tell him that Moses commanded that she should be stoned for her sin. When they speak to him about this, he mysteriously writes on the ground. After they persist, he tells them, "Let anyone among you who is without sin be the first to throw a stone at her" (v 7). Beginning with the elders, they all leave, and when Jesus is alone with her, he tells her, "Go your way, and from now on do not sin again" (v 11). Jesus' deliverance of this woman from death powerfully shows how he offers people everywhere new life and hope.

Preachers today will undoubtedly see a coherent word of inspiration emerging from these texts. In times when life seems as desolate as Jerusalem in the time of Jeremiah, in moments when people experience great suffering that leads them to despair, or in situations when it seems as though there is no way to escape the consequences of the guilt of sin, God offers people the gift of hope. Such an uplifting message as this is trustworthy, clear and sure.

Prayer: Thank you, God, for giving us the gift of hope in the midst of our despair. Amen.

Proper 20

Proper 20 may be used on the Sunday between September 18 and 24 (inclusive).

Jeremiah 36:1-4, 20-32

Psalm 119:81-88

2 Corinthians 1:23-2:11

John 8:21-30

The readings for this Sunday testify to how Gods' restorative power works in the lives of those who are broken or face losses. In Psalm 119 the author writes, "For I have become like a wineskin in the smoke, yet I have not forgotten your statutes" (v 83). With this metaphor, the psalmist testifies to the value of God's law despite the force of life's consuming flames. Such an image fits well with Jeremiah 36, which begins with God commanding Jeremiah, "Take a scroll and write on it all the words that I have spoken to you against Israel and Judah and all the nations, from the day I spoke to you, from the days of Josiah until today" (v 2). Jeremiah dictates this scroll to his scribe Baruch, and the completed scroll is delivered to King Jehoiakim of Judah. Because the scroll is written against Judah, it enrages the king, who burns it piece by piece in his fire and orders Jeremiah and Baruch's arrest. While the two are in hiding, God calls Jeremiah to write another scroll that includes the content of the first. "Then Jeremiah took another scroll," v 32 reads, "and gave it to the secretary Baruch, son of Neriah, who wrote on it at Jeremiah's dictation all the words of the scroll that King Jehoiakim of Judah had burned in the fire; and many similar words were added to them." In this way, God restores the prophet's voice, despite the destructive behavior of the king.

The theme of restoration is also echoed in today's Epistle reading. In 2 Corinthians 2, Paul tells the people in Corinth that he wants to spare them from having a painful visit with him. "I wrote you," he says, "out of much distress and anguish of heart and with many tears, not to cause you pain, but to let you know the abundant love that I have for you" (v 4). Apparently, the Corinthians went through a painful time when they followed through on Paul's recommended punishment of the man (described in 1 Corinthians 5 in Proper 14) who was living with his father's wife. In this later letter, Paul says, "This punishment by the majority is enough for such a person; so now instead you should forgive and console him, so that he may not be overwhelmed with excessive sorrow" (vv 6-7). "Anyone whom you forgive," he then asserts, "I also forgive" (v 10). In this way, the man who was once excommunicated is now restored.

Today's Gospel reading offers preachers one final word on the theme of restoration. In John 8, Jesus talks about his death, saying, "When you have lifted up the Son of Man, then you will realize that I am he, and that I do nothing on my own, but I speak these things as the Father instructed me" (v 28). Of course, in John's Gospel, Jesus' death is not his end but points to his ultimate restoration in the resurrection of his body. This message of restoration connects all of today's readings, and preachers will find in them a message of grace and hope for those who have ever faced losses or felt lost.

Prayer: God, when we are broken and face losses, restore us, we pray. Amen.

Proper 21

Proper 21 may be used on the Sunday between September 25 and October 1 (inclusive).

Job 1:6-22
Psalm 119:89-96
2 Corinthians 8:1-6
John 8:31-38

Examples of faithfulness in times of destitution abound in the recommended readings for this day. The author of Psalm 119 writes, "If your law had not been my delight, I would have perished in my misery" (v 92). In today's Hebrew Bible reading, Job also finds himself descending into misery. At the beginning of the story, God says of Job, "There is no one like him on the earth, a blameless and upright man who fears God and turns away from evil" (v 8). God agrees, however, to allow Satan (an accuser or adversary, not the personification of evil that developed in later Christian theology) to test Job's faithfulness. Job then suffers the loss of his animals, servants and children, but despite this, he declares, "Naked I came from my mother's womb, and naked shall I return there; the Lord gave, and the Lord has taken away; blessed be the name of the Lord" (v 21). After Satan afflicts Job with disease, his misery escalates, but in today's text, he shows faithfulness in the midst of his loss.

The New Testament readings for today also provide stories of faithfulness in the face of suffering, hardship and sin. In 2 Corinthians 8, Paul praises a group of destitute Macedonian churches by saying, "During a severe ordeal of affliction, their abundant joy and their extreme poverty have overflowed in a wealth of generosity on their part. For, as I can testify, they voluntarily gave according to their means, and even beyond their means, begging us earnestly for the privilege of sharing in this ministry to the saints" (vv 2-5). Paul uses them as an example of faithfulness to encourage the Corinthians to continue their support of the church's ministry. In John 8, Jesus also encourages those who believe in him to remain faithful, especially when faced with the enslaving powers of sin. "If you continue in my word," he says, "you are truly my disciples; and you will know the truth, and the truth will make you free" (vv 31-32). In being freed *from* sin, Jesus' disciples are set free *for* faithfulness in the face of life's evil and suffering.

Today's readings reveal how vital it is for Christians to have faith in God. Parishioners who reflect on Job's story may connect his losses with their own to gain a new perspective on life. They may also gain fresh insights when they consider the plight of the impoverished Macedonians whom Paul praises. For the Macedonians, stewardship is about a commitment of faith, not money, and in the midst of their financial crises, they give their all because they believe in the cause. They have nothing left to lose, and when people are in that position, they often gain a sense of freedom that puts life's other problems into context. Preachers of today's texts have a wonderful opportunity to testify to the gift of freedom that comes from faith.

Prayer: God, help us to face life's evil, suffering, poverty and pain with the freedom that we find through faith in you. Amen.

Proper 22

Proper 22 may be used on the Sunday between October 2 and 8 (inclusive).

Job 3
Psalm 119:113-120
2 Corinthians 11:16-31
John 8:39-47

In today's readings, anger is addressed and expressed in surprising ways. The selection from Psalm 119 begins, "I hate the double-minded, but I love your law" (v 113). Throughout today's verses, the psalmist is angry with those who turn away from God's commandments. The anger of the apostle Paul is also apparent in today's reading from 2 Corinthians 11. He defends himself against those who accuse him of being foolish, boastful, inauthentic and weak. "Are they Hebrews?" he asks, "So am I. Are they Israelites? So am I. Are they descendants of Abraham? So am I. Are they ministers of Christ? I am talking like a madman - I am a better one: with far greater labors, far more imprisonments, with countless floggings, and often near death" (vv 22-23). In John 8, Jesus also defends himself. "Now you are trying to kill me," he says, "a man who has told you the truth that I heard from God" (v 40). Later, Jesus cries out, "You are from your father the devil, and you choose to do your father's desires" (v 44). While some may be offended by the angry tone in these readings, they may also discover the liberating truth that if it is acceptable for Jesus and Paul to get angry, then Christians are also free to experience and express anger.

The aforementioned readings address anger toward others, but today's text from Job 3 describes intense anger directed at God. After Job was faithful in the face of his losses in chapter 1, God agrees to allow Satan to afflict him with disease in chapter 2. In chapter 3, Job responds to his sickness with some of the deepest, most soul-searching words in the Bible. "Let the day perish in which I was born," Job laments, "and the night that said, 'A man-child is conceived'" (v 3). In the throes of his suffering, he cries out the anguished question, "Why did I not die at birth, come forth from the womb and expire?" (v 11). In effect, Job is asking the timeless question that if God is all loving, good and powerful, why is there such unjust suffering and evil in this life.

While there is no good answer to this question, preachers will see in today's readings the truth that anger is an acceptable human emotion and that God is able to deal with it. Job's response to his pain is engaging because it is so authentically human. There are times when many people can identify with Job's wish that he had never been born, and the Bible gives voice to these feelings. Even though many Christians find it hard to own and express their anger toward others or God, today's readings help preachers and parishioners alike to do so in faithful and authentic ways.

Prayer: God, help us to accept the anger that arises from life's pain and injustice. Help us also to know that you are able to deal with the anger we feel toward you. Amen.

Proper 23

Proper 23 may be used on the Sunday between October 9 and 15 (inclusive).

Job 40:15-41:11
Psalm 119:121-128
2 Corinthians 13:5-10
John 8:48-59

The theme of testing is a common thread that runs through today's readings. Some of the selections reveal how people test

God. In Psalm 119, the author writes, "It is time for the Lord to act, for your law has been broken" (v 126). The psalmist witnesses people testing God by breaking the law and calls on God to decisively respond with justice. In John 8, Jesus is tested by a group of religious leaders, to whom he says, "Very truly I tell you, whoever keeps my word will never see death" (v 51). When they hear this, they accuse him of having a demon and ask, "Are you greater than our father Abraham, who died? The prophets also died. Who do you claim to be?" (v 53). He responds by saying, "Your ancestor Abraham rejoiced to see my day; he saw it and was glad" (v 56). When they angrily ask how a man under fifty years of age has seen Abraham, he says, "Very truly, I tell you, before Abraham was, I am" (v 58). They are so outraged by his claim that they gather stones to hurl at him, but he escapes.

Today's remaining readings in 2 Corinthians 13 and Job 40 and 41 emphasize how God helps people endure times of testing. Paul, for instance, encourages the Corinthians to examine themselves to see if they are living in right relationship with each other and God. Paul demonstrates this by examining himself and confessing that even though some may judge his ministry to be a failure, he hopes that they will find that he passed the test. Job also is severely tested and bitterly complains about the agony and the injustice of his suffering. In today's selection, God responds to Job's complaints by appearing to him in a whirlwind and telling him to think about the hippo and the crocodile. (God is actually not just referring to ordinary animals, but to giant creatures of mythological proportions as described in Psalms 74 and 104 and Isaiah 27). While this also might sound unhelpful, God is really inviting Job to set his suffering in a cosmic perspective and to see the glory of creation along with the suffering that exists in it. In the book's final chapter, Job's deference to God shows that he has learned from the trials he experienced in chapters 1 and 2, and when he looks outward by praying for his friends, he discovers that his fortunes and relationships are restored.

The readings for this day show that while it is futile to test God, God helps people throughout life's challenges. In times of suffering, some people over simplify 1 Corinthians 10:13 and offer the cliché that God does not give people more than they can bear. Today's scriptures, however, teach the greater truth that God helps people to face hardships when they are unable to do so themselves.

Prayer: God, help us not to put you to the test. See us through every test in life, we pray. Amen.

Proper 24

Proper 24 may be used on the Sunday between October 16 and 22 (inclusive).

Ecclesiastes 1:3-11
Psalm 119:145-152
James 1:2-11
John 10:31-42

The Bible texts for today speak about the transience of life, in contrast to the eternal character of God. Today's readings in Ecclesiastes and James both focus on the fleeting nature of life. While the book of Ecclesiastes appears only twice (once as an optional reading) on Sundays in the *RCL*, it is one of the most remarkable writings in the Bible. Authored by Koheleth, known also as "The Teacher" (or "The Preacher"), it advances the Hebrew Bible progression further into wisdom literature. Today's selection from Ecclesiastes 1 begins with Koheleth asking, "What do people gain from all the toil at which they toil under the sun?" (v 3). He answers this rhetorical question by describing the passing of human generations, the rising and setting of the sun, the circuitous blowing of the wind and the flowing of streams into an eternally hungry sea. Through these examples, he shows how the attainments of this world are weary and fleeting. This theme of transience also appears in today's Epistle reading, which moves from Paul's letters to that of James. In his first chapter, James writes, "For the sun rises with its scorching heat, and withers the field; its flower falls, and its beauty perishes" (v 11). While James' metaphors describing transience are similar to those of Koheleth, James is different in that he uses them to warn his readers to avoid temptations such as doubt and greed.

The remaining readings address the theme of how humans, though transient, participate in God's gift of eternal life. In Psalm 119, the author writes, "Long ago I learned from your decrees that you have established them forever" (v 152). Not only does scripture describe the endlessness of God's law, but it also speaks (particularly in John) of how people share in the promise of eternal life. In John 10, a crowd want to stone Jesus for blasphemy because they hear him as claiming to be God. Jesus alludes to Psalm 82:6 when he answers them by saying, "Is it not written in your law, 'I said, you are gods?' If those to whom the word of God came were called 'gods' - and the scripture cannot be annulled - can you say that the one whom the Father has sanctified and sent into the world is blaspheming because I said, 'I am God's Son?'" (vv 35-36). By identifying people (especially himself) with "gods," Jesus is showing how human beings, though transient, participate in the life of divinity, which is timeless and eternal.

One of the most difficult realities of pastoral ministry, and of life in general, is the fact that people enter each other's lives, make impacts on them, and then for varying reasons, leave. Everyone's stay on earth is temporary, and one of the great challenges of ministry is dealing with the sense of loss people feel because of life's changes. While today's scriptures highlight the transient nature of life, Jesus points to a dimension beyond the temporal to which all people are called.

Prayer: God, help us to glimpse the eternal in the midst of the transience of life. Amen.

Proper 25

Proper 25 may be used on the Sunday between October 23 and 29 (inclusive).

Ecclesiastes 2:1-11
Psalm 119:153-160
James 2:18-26
John 11:47-53

The recommended readings for today show that human works are important but also limited. Psalm 119 continues to emphasize the importance of doing the works of the law. "Look on my misery and rescue me," the psalmist writes, "for I do not forget your law" (v 153). Also, today's selections from Ecclesiastes and James address the theme of human works in different yet remarkable ways. In Ecclesiastes 2, Koheleth writes, "I made great works; I built houses and planted vineyards for myself" (v 4). As he assesses his accomplishments, however, he concludes, "Then I considered all that my hands had done and the toil I had spent in doing it, and again, all was vanity and a chasing after wind, and there was nothing to be gained under the sun" (v 11). While Koheleth's acts are displays of self-indulgence, the works James describes are good deeds that in his view are inextricably linked to faith. James insists that faith cannot be shown apart from works, declaring, "You see that a person is justified by works and not by faith alone" (v 24). While these writers both speak philosophically on the subject of human action, they are radically different in their understanding and interpretation of it.

The selection from John 11 places the subject of human works in the framework of God's greater plan for all people. After Lazarus' resurrection, the chief priests and Pharisees call a meeting of the council because they are afraid that if people continue to believe in Jesus, the Romans will come and destroy not only the temple but all Israel. Caiaphas, the high priest, offers a concise argument for killing Jesus and (apparently unintentionally) a rationale for the broader purpose of Jesus' act on the cross. "You know nothing at all!" he exclaims. "You do not understand that it is better for you to have one man die for the people than to have the whole nation destroyed" (vv 49-50). The narrator of John then explains, "He [Caiaphas] did not say this on his own, but being high priest that year he prophesied that Jesus was about to die for the nation, and not for the nation only, but to gather into one the dispersed children of God" (vv 51-52).

While Biblical authors differ on the value they place on human works, Christian theology places the utmost emphasis on Jesus' act of self-giving love on the cross. Debates over the role of faith and of the efficacy of works in being justified, sanctified and saved all take their place before the cross, which, for Christians, puts the faith and work of all people in proper perspective. Preachers will do well to be attuned to this truth as they work with these texts.

Prayer: We pray, God, that we might praise you with our faith and works as we celebrate how your act of self-giving love on the cross delivers us from evil and death. Amen.

Proper 26

Proper 26 may be used on the Sunday between October 30 and November 5 (inclusive).

Ecclesiastes 7:1-14
Psalm 119:161-168
James 4:11-17
John 11:55-57

As the liturgical year of the church nears an end, the theme of death appears in today's readings. In Ecclesiastes 7, Koheleth writes, "It is better to go to the house of mourning than to go to the house of feasting; for this is the end of everyone, and the living will lay it to heart" (v 2). He continues by saying, "Better is the end of a thing than its beginning; the patient in spirit are better than the proud in spirit" (v 8). In this passage, Koheleth sees death not so much as a tragedy to be avoided as a reality to be accepted. While James is also philosophical about death, he differs from Koheleth in that he views human mortality as a warning not to take things in life for granted. In today's selection, he begins by warning his readers against judging one another and then exhorts them not to speak as though life tomorrow in this world is guaranteed. "What is your life?" he asks. "For you are a mist that appears for a little while and then vanishes. Instead you ought to say, 'If the Lord wishes, we will live and do this or that.'" (vv 14-15). For James, death makes all human activity provisional, and because of this, people should be wary of boasting and all wrongdoing.

While Koheleth and James present death as a fact that affects human living, the Bible is not silent on its tragic aspects. "Princes persecute me without cause," the author of Psalm 119 begins in today's selection, "but my heart stands in awe of your words" (v 161). Today's Gospel reading in John 11 describes the persecution that will eventually end in Jesus' death. It sets the stage for the

Passover festival in Jerusalem where Jesus will conclude his earthly ministry. John writes, "Now the chief priests and the Pharisees had given orders that anyone who knew where Jesus was should let them know, so that they might arrest him" (v 57). Jesus' arrest, of course, leads to his crucifixion, and preachers who read the final part of this passage slowly and deliberately will emphasize the tragic reality that awaits Jesus at this Passover.

In worship services this time of year, many Protestant churches recognize Reformation (Reconciliation) Day on October 31 and (with Roman Catholic churches) All Saints' Day on November 1. These congregations often observe the Sunday that falls on this day as a "Memorial Sunday" during which they light candles, chime bells or in other ways commemorate those who have died in their churches or communities. Because of this, today is an appropriate time for preachers to address the subject of death from the different perspectives shared in today's readings. As the days shorten and flowers and foliage begin to die in the northern hemisphere, these recommended readings have much to offer parishioners who are remembering deceased loved ones and confronting their grief this day.

Prayer: God, we pray that the reality of death might teach us about how we should live. We also ask for help with our grief, as we mourn the passing of our loved ones. Amen.

Proper 27

Proper 27 may be used on the Sunday between November 6 and 12 (inclusive).

Ecclesiastes 11:1-6
Psalm 119:169-176
Acts 27:1-2, 7-38
John 12:37-43

The scriptures for this Sunday show how important faith is in difficult times. In the last verses of Psalm 119, the author looks to God for deliverance. Today's selection begins, "Let my cry come before you, O Lord; give me understanding according to your word" (v 169). The remaining verses in the psalm appeal for help in similar ways. In today's reading from John 12, Jesus addresses a crisis of faith in the lives of those around him. John writes, "Although he [Jesus] had performed so many signs in their presence, they did not believe him" (v 37). Because they lacked faith, they failed to discern Jesus' true identity. Faith is also an essential part of the wisdom offered in Ecclesiastes 11. "Send out your bread upon the waters," Koheleth writes, "for after many days you will get it back" (v 1). The author is describing a sower casting seeds on flooded fields. After the water recedes, the rich soil underneath produces abundant crops. Throwing seeds on water may look foolish, but the sower shows wisdom by having faith in the action's final outcome. Koheleth uses this and other agricultural images in today's selection to show the wisdom of well-placed faith.

From the floods of Ecclesiastes 11 to the stormy seas of Acts 27, faith is again shown to be essential in facing life's challenges. The stories of the storm at sea and shipwreck in Acts 27-28 mark the climactic end of the book of Acts and are among the greatest stories of faith ever told. Acts 27 begins as Paul and other prisoners set sail aboard a ship bound from Caesarea to Rome.

They stop at Crete, and Paul advises them not to continue. They ignore him, and after they leave, a violent storm arises. Paul tells them that they should have listened to him but also says that they will eventually make it to Rome. As the storm rages, they draw near to land and are afraid of wrecking the ship on rocks. They put down four anchors, and when some try to escape, Paul says, "Unless these men stay in the ship, you cannot be saved" (v 31). After going fourteen days in suspense without eating, Paul tells them to take some food. "After he had said this," Luke writes, "he took bread; and giving thanks to God in the presence of all, he broke it and began to eat" (v 35).

While today's readings all address the importance of faith, this last story is a parable of the church that speaks volumes about how necessary it is in hard times. Acts 27 is a crisis manual for Christians, urging them, when the seas are rough, to stay in the boat (the church) and share table fellowship (Holy Communion) together. Today in the church, many anxiously want to jump ship for a place where they think seas will be calmer. A survival mentality is eroding churches' wills to weather storms, and sadly, fear all too often eclipses faith. Preachers and other leaders will be wise to hold onto this text as an example of how God calls people to be faithful and to trust that Jesus guides the church, even in the most disastrous of storms.

Prayer: God, help us to weather life's storms by having faith in you. Amen.

Proper 28

Proper 28 may be used on the Sunday between November 13 and 19 (inclusive).

Ecclesiastes 12
Psalm 144:1-8
Acts 27:39-28:10
John 12:44-50

As this book approaches its end, today's readings show how God delivers people from the ravages of time. The patterns of progressions that have been followed in Ordinary Time conclude today, and next Sunday's observance of the Reign of Christ heralds a new beginning. The Psalm and Hebrew Bible progressions close with poetic reflections on time's passing. In Psalm 144, the author writes, "O Lord, what are human beings that you regard them, or mortals that you think of them? They are like a breath; their days are like a passing shadow" (vv 3-4). Ecclesiastes 12, one of the most beautiful elegies about old age that has ever been written, speaks even more eloquently to this point. This passage contains striking geriatric images of eye disease (v 2), hand tremors (v 3) osteoporosis (v 3), decaying teeth (3), failing vision (v 3), loneliness and isolation (v 4), hearing loss (v 4), shallow sleep (v 4), fears of falling (v 5), fears of victimization (v 5), lightening hair (v 5), lagging sexual desire (v 5) and finally, death (v 5). Although Koheleth conveys a powerful sense of transience with these words, the book concludes by pointing to the eternal. "The end of the matter;" he writes, "all has been heard. Fear God, and keep his commandments; for that is the whole duty of everyone. For God will bring every deed into judgment, including every secret thing, whether good or evil" (vv 13-14).

Today's Gospel and New Testament readings further demonstrate how God saves people from time's wreckage. The selection from John 12 is a summary of Jesus' teaching in which he says, "I do not judge anyone who hears my words and does not keep them, for I came not to judge the world but to save the world" (v 47). Jesus' teaching on eternal life in this passage shows that he is ultimately pointing to a reality that is beyond and outside of time. This truth is highlighted in the conclusion of last week's story from the book of Acts. In chapter 27, the ship carrying Paul wrecks near an island, but everyone on board makes it safely ashore. In chapter 28, while on the island that they learn is called Malta, Paul is bitten by a poisonous viper. When he shakes it off into a fire and is unharmed, the natives think he is a god. Because there are no snakes on Malta (and were none there in Paul's lifetime), Christians are wise to view this not as a literal historical event but as a parable of the church. By sharing this story, Luke shows that even the powers of death are helpless against the life-giving message of the gospel.

One of the most difficult truths of being human is that time moves inexorably forward. There is no way to pause, stop or rewind it, and it inevitably leads to death and decay. While today's scriptures do not deny this fact, they point to a reality that transcends existence in this world. As the church year nears its end, preachers will serve their congregations well by directing them to this truth.

Prayer: Deliver us, God, from the devastations of time. Amen.

Reign of Christ Sunday/Proper 29
Daniel 1:1-17
Psalm 9:1-8
Revelation 1:9-18
Luke 17:20-21

The readings for Reign of Christ Sunday contain kingly themes and bring *Beyond the Lectionary* full circle. The year ends where it begins, and today's texts from Daniel and Revelation set the stage for the selections found at the opening of this book (from Daniel 2 and Revelation 3, respectively). In Daniel 1, Belteshazzar (Daniel), Shadrach (Hananiah), Meschach (Mishael) and Abednego (Azariah) enjoy the benefits of serving King Nebuchadnezzar of Babylon. Daniel, however, asks the guard not to give them the royal rations to eat, but instead, only vegetables. After ten days of their vegetarian diet, Daniel and his friends are shown to be in better health than other servants of the king. In Revelation 1, Jesus appears to John of Patmos as a royal figure. John writes, "Then I turned to see whose voice it was that spoke to me, and on turning I saw seven golden lampstands, and in the midst of the lampstands I saw one like the Son of Man, clothed with a long robe and with a golden sash across his chest" (vv 12-13). John continues to describe Jesus as a ruler who is so powerful that he even holds the keys to Death and Hades.

Today's other readings also possess royal motifs. In Psalm 9, the author writes, "But the Lord sits enthroned forever, he has established his throne for judgment" (v 7). While a person seated on an earthly throne contrasts with Jesus' ministry as it is presented in the Gospels, Jesus does speak powerfully about God's kingdom in today's brief selection from Luke 19. Luke writes, "Once Jesus was asked by the Pharisees when the kingdom of God was coming, and he answered, 'The kingdom of God is not coming with things that can be observed; nor will they say, "Look, here it is!" or "There it is!" For, in fact, the kingdom of God is among you'" (vv 20-21). When Jesus says this, he is not speaking of some secret knowledge that will be unearthed by individualistic introspection. Instead, he is calling attention to himself, showing his followers that the kingdom is in *him*. It is not by looking inward, then, but by looking outward to Jesus that his followers witness the realm of God.

The patriarchal imagery of Christ the King as the powerful Lord of the kingdom of God is problematic for many people in the twenty-first century. Monarchy as it was practiced in ancient times (where rulers held absolute, dictatorial power) is now not only an archaic form of government in much of the Western world but is also an institution that carries negative and oppressive connotations for many people. Rulers who possess such power are often far from the ideals that most people would ascribe to God. Many Biblical texts that use this imagery, however, do so in an attempt to contrast God with the rulers of the world. The latter are corruptible and sadly, often use their power for evil. God, in contrast, works for good. In a time when Americans celebrate the holiday of Thanksgiving, preachers may indeed express gratitude for the realm of God as it is revealed in these final recommended readings.

Prayer: Thank you, God, for revealing your realm of love at work in our world. As this church year comes to an end, may it become for us a time of new beginnings. Amen.

Circle Books

Circle is a symbol of infinity and unity. It's part of a growing list of imprints, including o-books.net and zero-books.net.

Circle Books aims to publish books in Christian spirituality that are fresh, accessible, and stimulating.

Our books are available in all good English language bookstores worldwide. If you can't find the book on the shelves, then ask your bookstore to order it for you, quoting the ISBN and title. Or, you can order online—all major online retail sites carry our titles.

To see our list of titles, please view www.Circle-Books.com, growing by 80 titles per year.

Authors can learn more about our proposal process by going to our website and clicking on Your Company > Submissions.

We define Christian spirituality as the relationship between the self and its sense of the transcendent or sacred, which issues in literary and artistic expression, community, social activism, and practices. A wide range of disciplines within the field of religious studies can be called upon, including history, narrative studies, philosophy, theology, sociology, and psychology. Interfaith in approach, Circle Books fosters creative dialogue with non-Christian traditions.

And tune into MySpiritRadio.com for our book review radio show, hosted by June-Elleni Laine, where you can listen to authors discussing their books.

MySpiritRadio